CHAMBERS'S ELEMENTARY SCIENCE READERS (BOOK I)

LECTOR HOUSE PUBLIC DOMAIN WORKS

CHAMBERS'S ELEMENTARY SCIENCE READERS
(BOOK I)

VARIOUS

9 789356 146846
ISBN: 978-93-5614-684-6

Published: 1912

LECTOR HOUSE

LECTOR HOUSE LLP
E-MAIL: info@lectorhouse.com

'Here comes the big black hen.'

(*Page* 62)

CHAMBERS'S ELEMENTARY SCIENCE READERS (BOOK I)

WITH OBJECT LESSONS AND ILLUSTRATIONS

1912

CONTENTS

Page

(The Titles of Poetical Pieces are in *Italics*.)

OBJECT LESSONS.

CHAMBERS'S ELEMENTARY SCIENCE READERS

He sat down on the rug with her.

THE CAT.—PART 1.

walk′-ing	**thought**	**knew**	**sheaths**
watched	**stroked**	**smooth**	**won′-der**
ground	**fore′-paws**	**yawn**	**mis-take′**
shak′-ing	**toes**	**stretched**	**claw**

1. Pussy came walking along the garden-path. Harry watched her, and saw that she did not like the damp ground.

2. She jumped over the pools, and then began to run, shaking her paws as she got to the house.

3. 'Now, a dog does not mind wet feet,' Harry thought; 'he will go into the water, but Pussy will never go into the water.

4. 'She does not even use water to wash herself. Come here, Pussy! You don't like to wet your nice fur, do you?'

5. As Harry was always kind to pussy, she let him pick her up and carry her into the house.

6. He sat down on the rug with her, and stroked her glossy back. One of her fore-paws rested on his hand, and he began to look at it.

7. 'Here are five toes,' he said, 'but what funny toes they are!' He gently turned the paw over, and saw the sharp nails drawn in under the fur.

8. The cat knew that he would not hurt her, so she kept her claws in, and let him feel them on the outside.

9. He found under the paw a soft smooth pad. 'Now I know how it is that she can walk so softly!' he said. 'This must help her to walk in that way.'

10. Here pussy gave a great yawn, and stretched out both her paws, claws and all. Harry saw the sharp nails like hooks, and watched them go back into their sheaths. Then she curled herself up on his lap.

11. He took hold of one of her hind-feet, and found only four toes upon it. 'I wonder if this is a mistake,' he said, 'or if the other one is the same.' Yes, it was just the same: there were four toes, with a claw at the end of each.

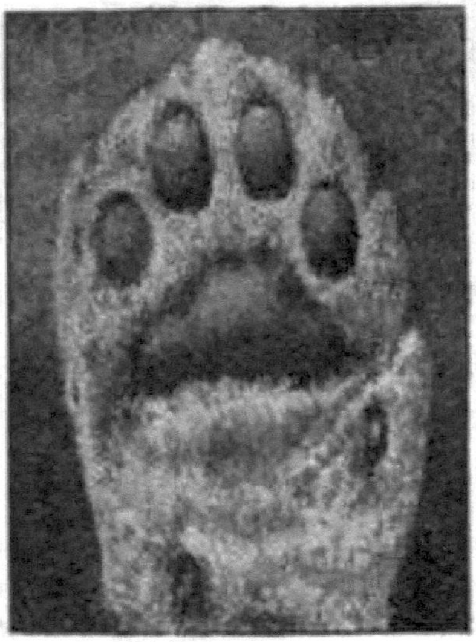

Cat's Paw.

THE CAT.—PART 2.

knives	**poured**	**touch**	**coun´-tries**
bot´-tom	**clean**	**rough**	**peo´-ple**
should	**sauc´-er**	**kit´-chen**	**thought**
tear´-ing	**tongue**	**cous´-ins**	**be-lieve´**

1. 'What long sharp teeth she has got!' cried Harry, as pussy sat up and opened her mouth. 'They look like knives. There are two at the top, and two at the bottom!

2. 'I should not like my finger to be in the way when you shut your mouth. Your teeth must be for tearing and cutting: I am sure you do not chew your food as I have to do.

3. 'And what a way you have of drinking!

'Here, pussy, would you like some milk?' said Harry, and getting up, he poured a little milk into a clean saucer.

4. The cat ran to it, and Harry went down on the floor close by to watch her drinking it.

5. He saw that pussy's tongue was not smooth like his own, but had tiny points all over it. It came into his mind that she had once licked his face, and her tongue had a 'scrapy' feeling.

6. 'Do it again, pussy, dear,' he said, but she went on lapping up the milk.

'May I touch your tongue, then, with one of my fingers?'

7. But pussy did not like this. Then Harry took a drop or two of the milk into the palm of his hand. And when the cat had taken all she had in the saucer, she came and licked up the milk in his hand.

8. She went on licking even when all was gone, and Harry was able in this way to feel how rough her tongue was.

9. Just then his mother came into the kitchen, and Harry told her what he had been doing.

She asked:

'Have you looked at pussy's eyes?'

10. 'They are funny eyes,' he said; 'they are green, but there is not much of them to be seen.'

'Not just now,' said his mother, 'but she can open them wide when she likes. Then she can see even in the dark.'

11. 'In the dark, mother? Well, she is not a bit like me!'

'No, she is not like you. But she has plenty of cousins. Her cousins are the big lions and tigers, that live in hot countries, and eat sheep and horses, and even people when they can get them.'

12. Harry thought a little, and then said: 'If I were as small as pussy is now, and if pussy were as big as I am now, I believe she would eat me!'

THE DOG.

fol´-lowed	**win´-dow**	**watched**	**Ber´-nard**
moth´-er	**noise**	**friend**	**shep´-herd**
hun´-gry	**la´-zy**	**bur´-ied**	**wrong**
lone´-ly	**be-cause´**	**e-nough´**	**talk´-ing**

1. A poor lost dog followed Harry and his little sister home from school, and tried to come into the house.

2. They shut the door; but, when they opened it again, the dog was still there.

3. He looked so sad that they begged their mother to give him some food. Then they said: 'We can't turn him out again to be hungry and lonely! Let us keep him till some one comes for him.' And very soon all three were happy at play in the garden.

4. The cat sat up on a window-sill, and looked at them. She did not seem to like the fun. What a noise they all made!

5. 'How much nicer he is to play with than pussy!' said Dora. 'He is not nearly so lazy as pussy.

6. 'Look, he is wagging his tail with joy! Now, if pussy wags her tail, it means that she is cross. But I think I like her round face better than his sharp one.'

7. 'I don't,' said Harry. 'See how bright he is, and how he looks as if he would like to do something for us!'

8. 'That is because we have been kind to him. Hi, good dog!' and Dora threw her ball to the very end of the garden, and watched her new friend run after it.

9. 'Do you think, Harry,' she asked, 'that he would save us if we were buried in the snow?'

St Bernard Dog.

'No, he is not a dog of that kind, and is not big enough. The big St Bernard dogs save people when they are lost in the snow.

10. 'But all dogs are good for something. Look at the shepherd's dog.'

'What can he do?'

11. 'Oh, he is a wise fellow! He knows just where his master means the sheep to go, and, if they go the wrong way, he turns them back, and never hurts one of them. Why, the shepherd does nothing but walk on, telling the dog now and again what to do.'

The Sheep Dog.

12. Here a dog barked on the road outside, and the dog in the garden pricked up his ears and barked too.

'They are talking to each other,' said Dora.

BUTTERCUPS.

chil′-dren	**hun′-gry**	**piec′-es**	**mid′-dle**
flow′-ers	**bas′-ket**	**hair′-y**	**break**
dai′-sy	**ought**	**yel′-low**	**leaves**
chains	**but′-ter**	**threads**	**seeds**

1. One day the children were out in the fields, running races, picking flowers, and making daisy-chains!

2. When they began to feel tired and hungry, they got milk and cake out of mother's basket, and had a long rest on the dry, warm grass.

3. 'How these buttercups shine!' said Dora; 'they look like gold!'

'Gold-cups, they ought to be called, not butter-cups,' said Harry. 'They look like cups, don't they?'

4. 'But they would not hold water like real cups. Look at this one; it is in five pieces.'

5. 'Five? Oh yes! And look underneath. There is another sort of cup with five leaves in it.'

'Only it is not bright and golden, but green and hairy.'

6. 'Now, you found that out, and I found the five yellow leaves. It is my turn again. I can see yellow threads standing up in a ring all round the middle of the cup, and their tops are thick.'

7. 'It is my turn now! In the very middle there is a green heap. It looks as if the yellow threads were taking care of it.'

'Oh, the heap is all made up of little round things! Look, I can pull it to pieces.'

8. 'So can I,' said Harry; 'here is one, here is another! They are not round after all, do you see? Each is round at the bottom, but has a little bent horn at the top.'

9. 'They must be seeds. I will break one open. Oh no! Just look, there is a little ball inside. Have you found a ball in yours?'

'Yes, there is a ball in every one. It must be a seed, or a little egg.'

10. 'Birds have eggs,' said Dora, 'plants have seeds.'

'Well, it is all the same thing,' said Harry.

'I think the green thing with a horn is only a case to take care of the seed.'

Butter-cup.

11. 'All these things seem to take care of each other. First, the green leaves at the back take care of the yellow cup.'

'And the yellow cup takes care of the yellow threads.'

'And the yellow threads take care of the green cases.'

'And the green cases take care of the seeds.'

Daisies.

DAISIES AND BUTTERCUPS.

mead´-ows	**maid´-en**	**win´-ter**	**ground**
stalk	**light´-ly**	**cun´-ning**	**chil´-dren**
cov´-ered	**ten´-der**	**dai´-sy**	**moss´-y**
yel´-low	**tread**	**straight**	**but´-ter**

I.

1. I'm a pretty little thing,
   Always coming with the spring;
   In the meadows green I'm found,
   Peeping just above the ground.
   And my stalk is covered flat
   With a white and yellow hat.

2. Little maiden, when you pass
   Lightly o'er the tender grass,
   Step aside and do not tread
   On my meek and lowly head;
   For I always seem to say,
   'Chilly winter's gone away.'

II.

1. I'm a cunning little thing,
Coming also with the spring.
Near the daisy I am found,
Standing straight above the ground;
And my head is covered flat
With a glossy, yellow hat.

2. Little children, when you pass
Through the tall and waving grass,
Do not pluck, but gently tread
Near my low and mossy bed;
For I always seem to say,
'Milk and butter fresh to-day.'

WHEAT.—PART 1.

field	**bas´-ket**	**grains**	**joints**
fa´-ther	**watched**	**east**	**be-lieve´**
wheat	**threw**	**morn´-ing**	**for´-est**
plough	**har´-row**	**earth**	**stalks**

1. There was a very little field at the bottom of the garden, and father made up his mind to grow wheat in it.

2. A friend kindly lent him a horse and plough, and the soil was quickly turned over. A few days afterwards the seed was sown.

3. The children helped to do this.

They got up very early one morning and went out with their father. Harry had a bag full of wheat, and Dora had a little basket.

4. They watched what their father did, then dipped their hands into the wheat, and threw it out over the earth.

5. After that, the horse came again with a harrow, to cover the seed over with soil, and it was left to grow.

6. It seemed strange to think that those little hard grains would grow up to be tall plants and have other grains upon them.

7. 'I hope we shall have some nice soft rain,' said father, as they left the field.

8. Many days went by, rain came again and again. There was sunshine, too; but sometimes the east winds blew.

9. Dora and Harry went out every morning to look at the field. But they always came in saying that there was nothing but brown earth to be seen.

10. At last, one morning they came in running and jumping. 'Our wheat is up! There are tiny green leaves all over the field!'

11. After this there was always something fresh to see. The wheat-plants grew taller, and put out long leaves.

12. Dora said one day that they looked like grass, and her mother told her that wheat was a large kind of grass.

'Look at the shape of the leaves,' she said, 'and the joints in the stems.'

13. The wheat soon grew so tall that it stood above the heads of the children. They used to go in among it, and make believe that they were lost in a great forest.

14. One day, when they were lost like this, they saw that the tops of the stalks had opened. Inside there were green stems with green ears upon them.

WHEAT.—PART 2.

heard	**seemed**	**truck**	**han′-dle**
talk′-ing	**sur-prise′**	**mean**	**min′-utes**
har′-vest	**rail′-way**	**flour**	**treat**
sup′-per	**heav′-y**	**lis′-ten**	**tea**

1. Every day the ears grew larger and harder, and then they began to look yellow.

2. The children, too, heard their father and mother talking about their golden grain, and saying it was ripe.

3. At last, one very hot day, they found that the time had come to cut the wheat. A kind friend came to help, and Harry and Dora and the new dog jumped about and ran in and out, and thought that they helped too.

4. The children talked much about their harvest, and mother made them a harvest-supper. What a day it was!

5. It seemed so odd to have a bin full of grain just like the grain they had sown in the spring.

6. And now there was a great surprise for them. A railway-man came with a heavy box on a truck, and when the box was opened, what do you think there was inside?

A mill—a fine new wheat-mill!

7. 'We do not need now to go to the miller!' said mother, looking very glad. 'We are going to have a miller in our own house—no, two millers, I ought to say!'

8. 'Two millers!' cried Harry.

'Do you mean Harry and me?' asked Dora.

'Yes, my dear children, I mean you. You are going to be my dusty millers!

9. 'I will show you how much you are to grind, just a little every day. You must put it into this big red pan, and cover it up, and when I want to bake I shall always have plenty of flour ready.

10. 'And listen! You shall have a penny each every week for doing the work.'

At this Dora and Harry jumped for joy, clapped their hands, and ran to their mother to hug her.

11. Then she put some of the wheat into the mill, took hold of the handle, and made the wheel go round. Harry next took his turn, and Dora hers, and in a few minutes they found in the box below a heap of nice soft flour.

12. 'Now,' said mother, 'let us give father a treat when he comes home! We will make some nice cakes with this flour, and have them for tea! Grind a little more, dear millers, while I make up the fire.'

SLATE.—PART 1.

rid′-dle	**won′-der**	**sup-pose′**	**smooth**
ex-act′-ly	**bought**	**fin′-gers**	**re-mem′-ber**
guessed	**Sat′-ur-day**	**met′-al**	**piece**

1. 'What is the oldest thing in this room?' asked the mother one day.

'Is this a riddle?'

'No, not exactly.'

2. Dora guessed one thing, and Harry another, and at last they gave up guessing. 'Unless,' said Harry, 'it is the fender, or the poker.'

3. 'It is very likely that the thing you were drawing on just now is older than any of those.'

4. 'That slate? Why, mother!' cried the children, opening their eyes wide with wonder, 'you bought it only last Saturday!'

'So I did. But it was not made last Saturday.'

5. 'No, I suppose the man cut it, and made the frame, and fixed it on before that.'

'Perhaps on Friday,' said Dora.

A Slate Quarry.

6. 'But the slate itself,' the mother went on, 'where did that come from? Did the man make it?'

Harry and Dora looked well at it, turned it over, rubbed their fingers on it, and said they did not know.

7. 'Well, would you say it is like wood, or like stone, or is it metal like the poker? Is it a kind of wood, do you think? Did it ever grow?'

'I think it must be a sort of rock, or stone,' said Harry, 'only very smooth and thin.'

8. 'The man who worked at it before it came to the shop made it smooth and cut it thin. It was not smooth and thin at first. But you are quite right; it is a sort of stone.'

9. 'It is as cold as a stone,' said Dora, putting it against her face. 'Do you remember, Harry, how cold our hands were in winter when we did sums? Yes, and it is very hard. I am sure it is a piece of rock.'

SLATE.—PART 2.

should	**laugh′-ing**	**set′-tled**	**weighted**
laughed	**pur′-pose**	**hap′-pened**	**through**
high′-er	**prop′-er-ly**	**deal**	**heaved**
thought	**please**	**dead**	**brok′-en**

1. 'I should like to see a rock all made of slate! Have you ever seen one, mother?'

'Yes, many, dear. But there are none near.' Then she laughed a little. 'But if you like to go just outside the door you will see rows and rows of slates.'

2. Out they ran, looked all over the ground, then at the garden-wall, then back at their mother, who had come to the door.

'Look at the house,' she said, 'look higher!'

3. 'Oh, we never thought of the roof,' they cried, and ran in again laughing. 'But those slates are not so nice and smooth as our slates.'

'Your slates are made smooth on purpose. Besides, they are made of better slate—older slate. The older the slate is the better it is.'

4. 'How old?'

'No one knows. It is a long story, and no one can tell it properly. Shall I tell you as much as I know?'

'Yes, do, please, mother!' and the two settled themselves at her feet.

5. 'Well,' she began, 'once upon a time there was a great stir at the bottom of the sea. The heat and gas under the ground broke through and pushed out everything that was in the way.

6. 'Stones, ashes, and dust came flying up through the water, and then fell back into the water again. When all was quiet, they settled down at the bottom of the sea, and became mud.

7. 'All this happened many times, till there was a great deal of mud. Then, little by little, the mud was covered up by other things.'

8. 'What sort of things?'

'Dead fish, perhaps, and shells, and sand and mud that had been brought by rivers into the sea. These things lay on the top of the mud and weighed it down.

9. 'The heat under the bottom of the sea still kept up, and made the mud very hot, and baked it through. At last it gave a great push, and heaved the mud up above the water, so that it became dry land.

10. 'In other ways it was made harder and harder, until it was turned into rock. And now we call it slate. Here is a bit of your old broken slate. See if you can turn it into mud again!'

CHALK.—PART 1.

a-cross′	**piece**	**wheat**	**earth**
morn′-ing	**teach′-er**	**col′-ours**	**brown**
chalk′-ing	**black′-board**	**fetch**	**moist**
picked	**spread′-ing**	**laughed**	**through**

1. A few days after this, Dora and Harry were going across the fields. They saw a horse and cart standing, and a man taking white stones out of the cart and putting them over the ground.

2. 'Why, it is Joe!' they cried, as they came nearer. 'Good-morning, Joe. What are you doing?'

'Chalking this bit of land, you see. You know what chalk is, do you?'

3. Harry and Dora picked up a piece or two.

'Teacher writes on the blackboard with chalk,' they said.

'Yes, you are right. It is used for many things,' and he went on spreading it over the field.

4. 'But what is it wanted here for, Joe?'

'No chalk, no wheat!' said Joe.

'Father put no chalk on our field, and we had such a heap of wheat!'

5. 'Yours is good land. This up here has never been used for farming. It had little old trees on it, you know, and they were cut down and their roots dug out of the ground; and now, look at it! It is poor soil.'

6. 'How do you know it is poor?'

'Look at the field below, what a nice brown it is! That will grow anything, but this is all colours—black, red, yellow, and green.

7. 'I have been a long way to fetch this chalk: I started off with old Dobbin this morning before it was light, and got it out of the chalk-pit.'

8. 'When we were fast asleep!' said Dora.

'Then you don't buy chalk at a shop?' said Harry.

Joe laughed.

'No; it comes out of the ground.'

'This is like the slate story,' said Dora.

Harry nodded.

9. 'But, Joe, I want to know how the chalk makes the ground good.'

'I don't know how, but it does. If it lies here for a year or more, the earth will turn brown, and we can grow wheat in it. Besides, chalk holds water, and so it will keep the ground moist up here.'

10. 'How?'

'Well, when it rains, the water will not run away through the earth, but will stay in the lumps of chalk. Are you going? Good-bye, then.'

'Fizz and bubble, bubble and fizz.'

CHALK.—PART 2.

eve´-ning	**air**	**hun´-dreds**	**catch**
brought	**stirred**	**smiled**	**died**
vin´-e-gar	**poured**	**crowds**	**dropped**
bub´-ble	**grains**	**threads**	**mixed**

1. The children had much to say that evening about Joe and the field. They had brought home a lump of chalk.

2. 'I will show you something,' said father, and he got a cup of vinegar, crushed a little of the chalk, and dropped it into the cup.

Fizz and bubble, bubble and fizz!

3. What was going on?

When the stir came to an end, the chalk was not there!

'Part of it has gone off in gas,' their father said. 'The rest is lime, and it is mixed with the vinegar.'

4. 'We did not see any gas,' said Harry.

'You can't see gas. It is like air. All those bubbles were made by the gas. It went out of the cup into the air.

'Now, get a cup of water. Come along! Where is your chalk?'

5. Father rubbed some of it into the water, and stirred it up. The water now looked like milk.

Father poured it into the sink, and showed Harry and Dora, at the bottom of the cup, a great many tiny grains.

6. 'Those little round things,' he said, 'are shells.'

'Shells!' said Dora, trying to see them better.

'Were live things ever in them?' asked Harry, and put a finger into the cup to fish some out.

7. 'Yes, long, long ago. That bit of chalk had hundreds and hundreds of shells in it. Now, mother, it is your turn! I have had mine. What do you know about chalk?'

8. Mother smiled and began: 'There was once a very deep sea, full of live things, little and big. And on the top of the water were crowds of tiny things in shells, that put out long arms like threads to catch their food.

9. 'When they died they all dropped to the bottom of the sea, and lay there. The shells were so very little that they made a sort of mud when they were mixed with the water.

'And now the mud is dry, and we call it chalk!'

THE MOUSE.

an′-i-mal	har′-vest	tail	squeak
noise	stalk	nib′-ble	hours
mouse	should	young	leaves
cheese	four	beasts	catch

1. Harry came running in one day to say that he had seen a little animal in the field.

2. 'It ran so fast, I could hardly see it. I looked a long time for it, and so did Dora, but we could not find it. Now, what do you think it could be, mother?'

3. Then in came Dora, 'It had a long tail, and was very little, and made no noise at all.'

4. 'It may have been a mouse,' said their mother; 'very likely it was.'

'But mice live indoors, do they not, and eat cheese, and run about in the walls, and make holes?'

5. 'How do you know all this?'

'I have heard them at grandmother's,' said Harry. 'Do they ever live out of doors?'

6. 'A good many do. There is a pretty little thing called a harvest-mouse. It makes a nest like a bird's, and hangs it up on a stalk of wheat.'

The Harvest Mouse and Nest.

7. 'I wish there had been one in our wheat!' said Dora. 'I should like to see the little nest and the baby-mice peeping out. They must be very, very small.'

8. 'Yes, the harvest-mouse is the very smallest four-footed animal we have. Then there is a field-mouse with a long tail, and a field-mouse with a short tail. Mr Short-tail likes to nibble at young trees.'

'Ah, that is not our mouse! He had a long tail.'

9. 'And then there is a wood-mouse.'

'Has he a short tail or long tail?' asked Harry.

'Long. I must tell you about a man who used to go out in the night in wild places to see what birds and beasts were doing when most of us were in bed.

10. 'One of the things he found out was that field-mice could sing!'

'Don't they squeak?'

'Yes; and he often heard them go on for hours making a kind of singing.

11. 'Sometimes they were close by him as he lay on the ground, and he would put out his hand to catch one. But when he opened it again it was full of grass or moss or leaves; and there was no mouse.'

'Did he never catch one?'

'Never.'

THE FIELD-MOUSE.

tum´-bles	**scarce´-ly**	**farm´-er**	**reared´**
ber´-ry	**weath´-er**	**stacks**	**un-der-neath´**
brown	**nib´-bling**	**treas´-ure**	**shad´-ow**
mer´-ry	**fruits**	**pleas´-ure**	**mead´-ow**

1. Where the acorn tumbles down,
Where the ash-tree sheds its berry,
With your fur so soft and brown,
With your eyes so soft and merry,
Scarcely moving the long grass,
Field-mouse, I can see you pass.

2. Little thing, in what dark den,
Lie you all the winter sleeping,
Till warm weather comes again?
Then once more I see you peeping
Round about the tall tree roots,
Nibbling at their fallen fruits.

3. Field-mouse, field-mouse, do not go,
Where the farmer stacks his treasure;
Find the nut that falls below,
Eat the acorn at your pleasure;
But you must not eat the grain,
He has reared with so much pain.

4. Make your hole where mosses spring,
Underneath the tall oak's shadow,
Pretty, quiet, harmless thing,
Play about the sunny meadow;
Keep away from corn and house,
None will harm you, little mouse.

'Oh, look at that one going into a hole.'

THE RABBIT.

moth´-er	**friends**	**morn´-ing**	**fight**
rab´-bits	**Sat´-ur-day**	**beat´-ing**	**meant**
dare´-say	**an´-i-mals**	**knock**	**dan´-ger**

1. Harry and Dora were coming home with their mother from a long walk, when they saw some rabbits playing about on the grass.

2. They wished to stay and watch them, and the three sat down on a log a little way off.

'Oh, look at that one going into a hole!' said Dora. 'See his funny tail. Why is he going into a hole?'

3. 'That is his house,' said their mother. 'I daresay he is sleepy and wants to go to bed.'

'He goes early, then, like the birds?'

'Yes, about sunset. He gets up a little before sunrise.

4. 'There goes another! They will soon all be gone.'

'Then we can look at their houses?'

'Only at their front doors. If you were to sit quite still over there in the day-time, you would see the rabbits popping in and out.

5. 'After a time they would find out that you were their friends, and then you would be able to watch their doings.'

6. Then mother told them more about the man who often stayed out all night to see what animals did. 'One morning, before it was quite light, he heard a tap-tap near him, and saw a rabbit beating on the ground with his hind-feet close to another rabbit's hole.

7. 'He saw him go to another hole and tap there, and then to another. Some holes he passed and did not knock at all.

'At last he had just begun tap-tapping in front of a hole, when out rushed a big rabbit. They began to fight, and they both rolled down to the bottom of the hill.

8. 'The man often saw rabbits tapping like this. Sometimes two or three would come out to speak to the one that tapped, and they seemed to have a friendly chat.

9. 'There was another sound they could make with their hind-feet. If one of them made it, the others would run into their holes as fast as they could. It meant danger.'

'What was it like?' asked Dora.

'*Tap-pat.*'

IVY.

win′-ter	**be-tween′**	**straight**	**thread**
vase	**pur′-pose**	**veins**	**ten′-der**
changed	**um-brel′-la**	**flow′-er**	**mouth**
sprays	**mid′-dle**	**thick′-er**	**use′-ful**

1. Some sprigs of ivy had been standing all the winter in a vase. The water had often been changed, and the leaves washed.

2. When spring came each spray began to put out buds. The buds were not all at the ends of the sprays, but came out also close to the old leaves.

3. At last there was a very small bud between every old leaf and the stem. When the first bud opened into a leaf, Dora and Harry clapped their hands, and called every one to look.

4. 'How clean and sweet it is!' cried Dora. 'And do you see something like wool or hair on it?'

'How curly it is!' said Harry. 'It is not quite open yet. Why, it is like a hand! All the leaves look rather like hands, don't they? See; one, two, three, four, five!'

5. 'Look at this old leaf against the light,' said the mother; 'now you can see the five long fingers. But people call them ribs, not fingers! They are for the purpose of keeping the leaf spread out.'

6. 'Like the ribs of an umbrella,' said Harry. 'They seem very strong; the middle one, which goes up straight from the stem, is the strongest of all.'

7. Dora was holding up one spray after another to the light. 'What are all these pretty marks on the leaves, mother, lines crossing about all ways?'

'Those are veins, dear. They carry the sap that feeds the leaves.'

8. 'What is sap?'

'The blood of plants and trees.'

'Oh,' said Dora, 'then that is the wet that comes out when I pick a flower or cut a leaf!

9. 'But look at this!' and she held up one of the sprays.

At the end of it was a little bunch of white, curly roots. Each root was not much thicker than a thread.

Spray of Ivy.

10. 'Don't touch them,' said the mother; 'roots are very tender things.'

'What is the good of them?' asked Dora.

'What is your mouth useful for?' asked her mother.

11. 'Oh, do you mean that the ivy eats and drinks?'

'Yes, that is what I mean. These roots take out of the water, or out of the earth, all sorts of things good for the food of the plant. They then send them up into the stem and on into the leaves.'

12. 'Mother,' said Harry, 'let us go and plant all this ivy. I am sure it wants to try the taste of the earth!'

A TREE.

rab´-bits	**spread**	**birch**	**caught**
shoots	**rough**	**beech**	**oak**
ta´-ble	**heard**	**branch´-es**	**found**

1. 'Let us go over to that log where we sat when we saw the rabbits,' said Dora to Harry.

2. 'All right! We can play at ship, and the grass shall be the sea.'

'Or we can have see-saw, if we can find some wood to lay across the log.'

3. They were soon at the log, and on it they sat down, and looked about them.

The log was the trunk of an old oak, and a little way off stood the stump, with many new shoots and leaves coming out all round it.

It is all marked in rings.

4. Dora went and stood on it, and called out that she was on a hill. She jumped off and on a few times, and then said it would make a good table, and they might have tea on it.

5. Harry found that the stump had roots that spread out all round for a long way.

'How thick and hard they are!' he said; 'come and feel this one!'

'It is not like the roots we saw on the ivy,' she said. 'Now look at the top of the stump. It is all marked in rings.'

6. 'In the very middle there is a little light spot, and then come dark rings, and then more rings outside. Father once told me these rings showed how old the trees were. And do you see lines coming away from the middle?'

7. 'They look like the rays of the sun, which I draw on my slate,' said Dora. 'What a rough coat this tree had! Come and feel the outside of the log.'

'That is the bark! I have heard father talk about bark.'

8. 'Well, I shall call it the coat. It is the tree's overcoat to keep him warm and dry. But trees do not all seem to have rough coats. Look at that one!' and she ran over to a little birch, and pulled off some of its thin bark.

9. 'I have found a fine tree!' cried Harry; and Dora came running to look at it.

Leaves of the Beech and the Oak.

10. It was a beech, with a great round smooth trunk and long strong branches. Harry jumped up and caught at a leaf or two, and then went to pick an oak-leaf. He laid them side by side on his hand and looked at them, and found they were not at all alike.

BRICKS.

stopped	**trow´-el**	**teach´-er**	**breaks**
emp´-ty	**struck**	**re´-al-ly**	**moulds**
mor´-tar	**picked**	**clay**	**nice´-ly**
sound	**size**	**win´-ter**	**ov´-en**

1. Two men were making a wall by the road-side, and Harry and Dora stopped to look at them.

2. Another man was going away with a horse and cart. The cart was empty, but it had been full of red bricks. The men were putting these bricks on the wall and making them fast with mortar.

3. Dora liked the sound which the trowel made when it struck against the wall. Harry picked up one of the bricks and looked at it, and then Dora must look at one too.

4. They found that the bricks were light and easy to lift. They also saw that they were all of the same size and shape, as if they had been made, and not dug out of the ground.

5. They did not like to ask the men about them, and so they put the bricks down, and set off on their way home.

6. As they went they met their teacher, who stopped and spoke to them, so Harry asked her to tell them what bricks really were.

7. 'I wish there were a brick-field near,' she said, 'and then we would go and see it! But I can tell you a little about it.

8. 'Bricks are made of clay, and clay is dug out of the ground. Men dig it before winter comes, and let it lie out all the winter, and the frost breaks it up nicely for them.

9. 'The next thing is to mix it well into a paste, and then it is put into moulds.'

'What are moulds?' Harry asked.

'Well, these moulds are like boxes with no bottom or top.'

'Only sides, then?' said Dora.

10. 'Yes, they have two long sides, and two short ones, and they hold the soft, wet clay.

'You may call them clay-puddings before they are put into the hot oven. When they are taken out, what do you think they are? They are bricks!'

A DONKEY.

bot′-tom	**fruit**	**ap-ple**	**feast**
lane	**this′-tles**	**car′-rot**	**win′-dow**
don′-key	**hedge**	**touch**	**shag′-gy**
load	**rough**	**mor′-row**	**tuft**

1. At the bottom of the lane lived a donkey. Harry and Dora knew him well. They often met him going to town with a load of fruit, and they saw him in the lane every day cropping the grass and thistles by the hedge-side.

2. He knew them, too, for they would stop to pat his rough sides, or give him an apple or a carrot.

3. They wondered how he could eat such prickly things as thistles. A horse would never touch them.

4. One day his master took him into the garden while he was working. He let Neddy go up and down the paths and crop the grass, which had grown long on the little grass-plot.

5. The donkey did not once try to get at the pears and apples; he did not even look at them.

6. His master was pleased, and said to his wife: 'It is quite safe to leave the gate open, and let Neddy come into the garden when he likes. I shall be away to-morrow, but you need not look after him. He will be all right.'

7. Next day, Neddy walked into the garden, found that no one was there, and began to eat the fruit. He had a good feast before his mistress saw him from the window.

8. Then he was driven out, and the gate was shut. After that he always had to find his dinner in the lane.

9. The children saw him one day feeding with a white horse that had come down from the farm, and they stopped to talk to them.

10. Then Dora said to Harry:

'They are like each other, and yet not like! Neddy has a shaggy coat.'

'And his mane is short, and stands up.'

'His ears are very long.'

'His tail is not like Snowflake's tail; and, see, it has a little tuft at the end of it!'

'And Snowflake is much taller.'

SHEEP.

chalk	hedge	chew´-ing	for-got´-ten
wheth´-er	tear´-ing	though	brought
earth	swal´-low	re-mem´-ber	mouth

1. The next time that Dora and Harry were out, they ran up to the place where they had met Joe. They wished to see how the chalk was getting on, and whether the earth was brown yet.

2. After that they went over a stile into a field where many sheep were feeding. The sheep began to move away when they saw the boy and girl coming.

3. Then said Harry: 'Let us try mother's plan of keeping quite still and letting them see that we don't want to hurt them.'

4. So they sat down under a hedge and looked at the sheep for a long time, and soon one and another began to come near, eating away at the grass.

5. 'I like that sound of tearing off the grass, don't you?' said Dora.

'Do you see they swallow it all at once?' said Harry. 'What would mother say to us if we ate without chewing?'

6. 'There is some chewing going on, though. Look over there!' and she showed him some sheep that were lying down in the grass.

7. 'Oh, now I know! Don't you remember, Dora, father told us once what the cow does. It was that day we had tea at the farm.'

8. 'No, I don't remember. We saw the cows milked, and I had some new milk in a glass. I don't think father told me!'

9. 'Yes, he did. You must have forgotten. He said that the cow sent her food down into a big bag inside, and then it went into a smaller bag, where it was rolled up into little balls. And when the cow lay down to rest, she brought them up into her mouth and chewed them well.'

10. 'I should think the sheep must be doing the same thing. Look at this fat one close by! She is just sitting down. Now watch!'

'Yes, I can see her chewing! How funny it is! They all look as if they liked it, don't they?'

THE SHEEP.

la´-zy	**clothes**	**scant´-y**	**mer´-ry**
pleas´-ant	**chil´-ly**	**com´-mon**	**wool´-ly**
dai´-sies	**dew´-y**	**brown**	**coat**

1. 'Lazy sheep, pray tell me why
In the pleasant fields you lie,
Eating grass and daisies white,
From the morning till the night?
Everything can something do;
Oh what kind of use are you?'

2. 'Nay, my little fellow, nay,
Do not serve me so, I pray:
Don't you see the wool that grows
On my back to make you clothes?
Cold and very cold you'd be,
If you had not wool from me.

3. 'True, it seems a pleasant thing,
To nip the daisies in the spring;
But many chilly nights I pass,
On the cold and dewy grass,
Or pick a scanty dinner where
All the common's brown and bare.

4. 'Then the farmer comes at last,
When the merry spring is past,
And cuts my woolly coat away,
To warm you in the winter's day.
Little Master, this is why
In the pleasant fields I lie.'

TURNIPS.

white	win′-ter	sor′-ry	pressed
ly′-ing	din′-ner	heard	meal
tur′-nip	read′-y	peo′-ple	mean
picked	but′-ter	bread	jok′-ing

1. 'What are those sheep eating over there, at the far end of the field? There is something white all over the grass. What can it be?'

'Chalk?' Dora asked.

'No, they never would be so silly! Let us go and see.'

2. Up they got, and away they went. They found that the white things lying about on the grass were bits of turnip.

Harry picked one up and looked at it. It was only a round rind: all the inside had been eaten out.

He took it home with him to show to his mother.

3. He took it home with him to show to his mother, and she said:

'I saw some bits like this that were shooting out green leaves when spring came. They had been lying out on the ground in the winter, yet there was so much life in them that they could grow again. But, come, wash your hands: dinner is ready, and I have something to tell you. We are going to have turnips for dinner!'

4. When Harry had his helping of turnips he said:

'Now I am a sheep!'

'No,' said Dora, 'the sheep don't boil their turnips, or mash them with nice butter.'

5. 'But raw turnip is very nice,' said her father. 'I have often eaten one out in the fields. I am not at all sorry for the sheep.'

6. 'I have heard,' said mother, 'that, when corn was very dear, people had to use turnips in making bread. They say the bread looked good, and kept well. The water was first pressed out of the turnips, and then they were mixed with wheat-meal.'

7. 'I wish you would make some, mother,' said Dora, 'just for fun, to see what it is like.'

'I will—some day.'

8. 'What did you mean, mother,' Harry asked, 'about water in turnips?'

'There is a great deal of water in turnips,' said mother.

9. 'Turnips are nearly all water,' said father.

'Now, father, you must be joking,' cried Harry.

'No, I am not. Am I, mother?'

Mother smiled, and said 'No.'

GREEN PEAS.—PART 1.

peas	**watched**	**half**	**with′-er**
flow′-ers	**thought**	**count′-ed**	**stayed**
ten′-drils	**pur′-pose**	**true**	**shin′-y**
un-rolled′	**but′-ter-flies**	**flow′-er**	**touched**

1. Dora was alone in the garden. She had played about till she was tired, when she found herself close to the bed of peas. She had seen her father sow the peas, and now there were tall plants with leaves and flowers and green tendrils.

2. Dora unrolled one or two of these tendrils, and then watched them roll up again. She thought:

'How funny it is of the plant to put these out on purpose to take hold of the sticks! And how pretty the flowers are! They look like little white butterflies. I will pull one open.'

Pea-flower.

3. She picked a flower, and sat down with it on the grass. Inside of it she found something long and green. This she opened, and saw a row of tiny green balls.

4. Not one of them was half as big as a pin's head. They were all in a row, and Dora counted seven of them.

She picked out each one and laid them on her hand to look at.

5. Then it came into her mind that these little mites of things must be baby-peas. And she felt sorry to think what she had done, for she could not put them back into their nest, and now they would never grow up to be big.

6. She told Harry about it next day, and he said, yes, it was very true. But he must pull open just one flower himself and see the peas inside; and so he did. There were six peas in his flower.

7. Every day after this, Dora and Harry came to look at the plants.

For a long time the flowers were very pretty. Then they began to wither. One by one they dropped off; but the inside part of each stayed on, looking green and shiny.

8. The children called these shiny green things bags, till they heard some one say that they were pods.

Sometimes they touched them. They soon began to feel the peas inside. The pods grew larger and fatter every day.

GREEN PEAS.—PART 2.

bas´-ket	won´-der-ful	weath´-er	su´-gar
shell´-ing	break´-ing	earth	starch
bas´-in	fair´-y	moist	earth
taught	hap´-pens	pea	sun´-light

Pea-pods.

1. At last, one sunny morning, mother came out with a basket and began to pick the pods. Harry and Dora wished to help her, and all three were soon at work.

2. Next, the shelling began. Mother had a basin in her lap, and the two chil-

dren sat close to her and shelled their peas into it.

3. They told her how they had shelled the baby-peas. She taught them how each plant was a living thing, and had a tiny plant inside of it, all ready to come out at the right time. This was very wonderful.

4. 'Did that big plant come out of one little pea?' cried Dora.

'I can't see a little plant inside,' said Harry, breaking one of the peas open.

5. 'Yet it is there, a fairy-plant, with a root, a stem, and two leaves. These leaves take up nearly all the room in the green ball. How would you like to have two or three of these peas to plant? There! I can spare you three each from to-day's dinner.'

6. The children were glad to have them. 'I wish we could see them grow,' said Dora. 'What happens, mother, when they are in the earth?'

7. 'Do you mean, How do they begin to grow? Well, the weather must be rather warm, and the earth moist, and the pea swells itself out till it bursts open its thin coat. The little root goes down to fasten it firmly in the ground, and to look for food. Then the little stem and the two leaves come up to get air and sunshine. That is how it begins.'

8. 'What food is there in the ground? What food do the roots find?'

'Lime and iron'——

'Iron!' cried Harry.

9. 'Yes, there is iron in green peas! There are sugar, too, and starch, and fat, and water, and other things. Some come out of the earth, some come out of the air and the sunlight, and some the plant makes for itself. Oh, it is a very clever plant! But all plants are clever, I think.'

IRON AND METAL.

pock´-ets	heav´-y	cop´-per	sup-pose´
mar´-bles	weight	thought	wheat
wrapped	light´-er	zinc	i´-ron
size	though	met´-als	ket´-tle

1. 'What have you in your pockets, father?' asked Harry, pulling at them. 'Nuts? stones? marbles?'

'Put your hand in, and find out. Here, Dora, you can try the other pocket.'

2. In went two hands, and out came little hard lumps, each wrapped in paper. The children laid them on the table in a row, and wanted to know what they were.

'What have you in your pockets, father?'

3. They were not nuts, nor marbles, and not quite like stones. They were all about the same size, but one was very heavy. Harry and Dora held it in their hands to feel how heavy it was.

4. 'That is a bit of lead,' said their father. 'Which do you think is the next in weight?'

'This red one. It is a good deal lighter, though!'

'That is called copper. Now, what comes next?'

5. They were not sure, but thought that iron came next, and then tin, and then zinc. Their father told them these names as they went on. He told them also that all these things were metals, and had been dug out of the earth.

6. 'Suppose we make a box to keep them in?'

'Oh yes!' cried both.

'And if we find any more things like these, we will put them in.

7. 'Would you put in a buttercup?'

'No, no!'

'Or a grain of wheat?'

'No, it is not at all like these.'

'Or a bit of slate?'

'I think so,' said Harry.

Dora was not quite sure.

8. 'Yes, we will put the slate into the box. It is not a metal, but it came out of the ground. Now, what do you say to this?' And he pulled out a lump that looked like earth and stone.

9. What could this be? It was iron, just as it had come out of the ground, with clay and earth about it.

10. 'Once upon a time,' said father, 'the kettle, and the poker, and the fender, all looked like this!'

THE FAIRY RING.

danc´-ing	**sea´-sons**	**sphere**	**au´-tumn**
fair´-y	**year**	**sum´-mer**	**tress´-es**
queen	**cir´-cle**	**glide**	**cheeks**

1. Let us dance and let us sing,
   Dancing in a merry ring;
   We'll be fairies on the green,
   Sporting round the fairy queen.

2. Like the seasons of the year
   Round we circle in a sphere;
   I'll be Summer, you'll be Spring,
   Dancing in a fairy ring.

3. Spring and Summer glide away,
   Autumn comes with tresses gay;
   Winter, hand-in-hand with Spring,
   Dancing in a fairy ring.

4. Faster, faster round we go,
   While our cheeks with roses glow,
   Free as birds upon the wing,
   Dancing in a fairy ring.

NEEDLES.—PART 1.

treat	**coils**	**stretched**	**mid′-dle**
hol′-i-days	**steel**	**straight**	**chop′-ping**
aunt	**wire**	**ma-chine′**	**dropped**
nee′-dles	**wrapped**	**un′-cle**	**e-nough′**

1. Harry and Dora once had a great treat.

They went in the holidays to stay with an uncle and aunt who lived at a town where needles were made. We may call it Needle-town.

2. While they were there, they were taken to the mills to see the needles made.

3. The first room into which they went was very warm. It was called the wire-room. A workman who was there told them that it was filled with hot air night and day, so that no damp should come in and spoil the steel.

4. All round the room coils of steel-wire were hanging. They were wrapped up in paper, but the man took some of them down and let them look in. They saw that one coil was of very thick wire, while another was of wire as fine as a hair.

5. 'One of these coils would be more than a mile long if it were stretched out straight,' the man told Harry. 'Would you like to take hold of this one?'

But Harry found it too heavy, and it was hung up again on the wall.

6. Then they went into another room, where a machine was cutting a coil of wire into bits.

'They are much too long for needles,' said Dora, softly, to her uncle; but one of the workmen heard her, and said:

7. 'So they are! Each bit is going to be two needles. The two ends are to be the points, and the heads lie in the middle of the wire.'

8. But no heads were to be seen yet. And the wire was not even straight, for it had long been rolled up in a coil. As the machine went on chopping, and the wire-strips dropped, a man picked them up and put them on a shelf in a sort of oven.

9. There they were kept till they were red-hot, and then they were soft enough to be made straight.

NEEDLES.—PART 2.

points	un′-cle	ham′-mer	watched
heads	block	al-lowed′	piece
eyes	heav′-y	laugh′-ing	sharp

1. The next thing that the children saw was a grindstone turning round very, very fast.

2. A man put the bits of wire into a thing which was fixed just over the grindstone, and both ends were quickly rubbed sharp.

'Now you see the points of the needles.'

3. 'Now you see the points of the needles,' said the man, as the wire came out again.

'But there are no heads yet!' said Harry.

'And no eyes!' said Dora.

'Well, come along to the stamping-room,' said their uncle.

4. In this room they found a block of stone that had iron on the top of it. Over it hung a heavy hammer. A man who stood there took one of the wires, put it on the block, and made the hammer come down upon it.

5. The moment the hammer went up again the wire fell into a pan, and the children were allowed to look at it.

6. Still there were no eyes or heads! All that could be seen were two little dents, one on each side of the middle of the wire.

7. 'But, look again!' said uncle. 'Don't you see a tiny dot in each dent? That is where the eye is going to be.'

8. In the next room they found a great number of boys at work.

'Oh, uncle,' said Harry, 'do you think I could come here and help to make needles?'

'You would soon be tired of it,' said his uncle, laughing.

9. They went up to one of the boys, and watched him for some time. He took some wires that had come from the stamping-room, and laid them on a piece of iron, but held the two ends in his hands.

10. Then a heavy thing with two hard, sharp, steel points under it came down on the middle part of the wires, and made two holes just where the dots had been.

'Now we see the eyes, at last!' cried Dora.

NEEDLES.—PART 3.

thread´-ing	**rough**	**ov´-en**	**break´-ing**
to-geth´-er	**edg´-es**	**sec´-ond**	**bench**
tooth´-comb	**nee´-dle**	**steam´-ing**	**ham´-mer**
smooth	**thought**	**e-nough´**	**straight**

1. They went on into another room. Here there were boys again! And what were the boys doing? They were threading the wires together.

2. When they were all strung together, they looked like a long tooth-comb. The heads were in the middle, and the points lay on either side.

3. The boys took them to some of the workmen, and these men made the middle part quite smooth. Rough edges had been left along the tiny dents, and had to be rubbed down.

4. When this was done, a man made a line along the middle of the 'comb,' and then gently bent it backwards and forwards till it broke right in the middle.

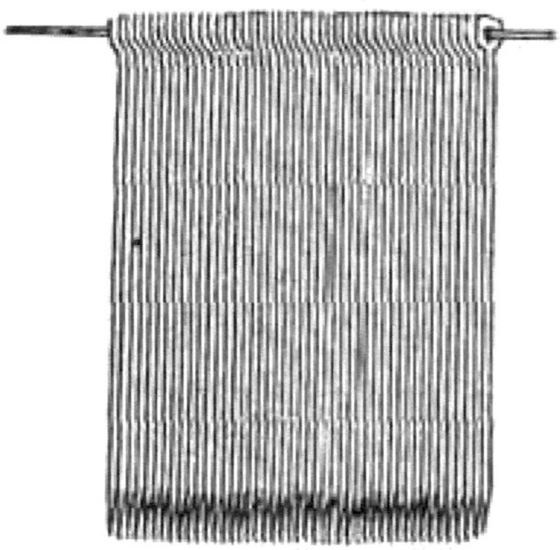

5. Harry and Dora were glad to see this. Each bit of wire looked like a needle now. It had a head of its own, and an eye, and a point.

6. The next thing was to make the needles hard. Dora and Harry thought they looked quite hard already, but they did not know.

7. How were they hardened? They were first laid on iron plates and put into a kind of oven.

'This is the second baking they have had,' said Harry.

They were kept in till they were white-hot.

8. When the needles came out, they were put into cold water! What a hissing and steaming they made! But they had to lie there till they were quite cool.

9. Then they were taken out and dried. The man said they were hard enough now, but something else must be done to them to make them able to bend well without breaking.

10. They were put on an iron plate over a fire, and gently moved about. Some of them curled up, and had to be taken off.

11. They were given to a woman, who was sitting on a bench with a little hammer in her hand and a small steel block in front of her. She laid a curly needle on the block, and hammered it till it was straight, and then another, and another.

NEEDLES.—PART 4.

clean′-ing	oil	man′-gle	Fri′-day
piece	em′-er-y	a-fraid′	points
can′-vas	pow′-der	brok′-en	hun′-gry
soap	bun′-dle	sec′-ond	laugh′-ing

1. The cleaning of the needles came next.

2. A great many were laid side by side on a piece of canvas, and covered with paste.

'What is the paste made of?' Harry wanted to know.

'Soft soap, my lad,' said the workman, 'and oil, and emery-powder.'

3. He rolled them all up in the canvas, tied string round the bundle, and put it between the rollers of a thing that looked like a mangle.

4. Dora and Harry opened their eyes wide. 'Think of needles being mangled! This will be something to tell mother!'

5. When the bundle was unrolled, they were afraid that the needles would be broken. But they were all right, and they were taken out and washed in warm soap-suds.

6. 'Now they must be clean!' said Dora.

'Not yet,' said the man; 'they have to be rolled up again with more paste, and put between those rollers again, and again, and again. It takes eight days to clean the best needles.

7. 'And it takes six days to clean the second-best,' said the man.

'Then even the second-best won't be done till Friday!' said Harry.

8. 'But we can go and see some needles that have been cleaned,' said his uncle. 'Let us go up-stairs again.'

9. And they went up into a room where many girls were sitting at a long table with heaps of bright needles before them. They were putting them in order, side by side, heads all one way, points another.

Dora was sure that she could not pick them out so quickly.

10. They were going on into another room to see the eyes of the needles made smooth, when Dora said, 'Oh, uncle, I am so tired!'

'So am I,' said Harry, 'and hungry, too.'

11. 'Come along, then,' said uncle, laughing. 'We all want our dinners, I think.' He took Dora's hand in his, and away they went.

THE KNIFE.

ro´-ley	**morn´-ing**	**blade**	**edg´-es**
po´-ley	**knife**	**han´-dle**	**rath´-er**
thought	**least**	**aunt´-ie**	**clock**

1. There was not much talking at dinner, till after the second helping of roley-poley.

2. Then Dora and Harry felt happy again, and began to tell their aunt all about the needle-making. She had seen it once, but it was a long time ago, and she thought she should like to see it again.

3. 'But if I had gone this morning,' she said, 'you would not have had your pudding.'

'That would have been sad,' said Dora.

4. 'What a lot of steel we have seen,' said Harry. 'I never knew there was so much in the world.'

5. 'You can see some on this table now.'

'Where?'

'What have I cut the pudding with?'

'Oh, the knife! Yes, I see; that must be steel; at least, that part of it. What do you call that part?'

'The blade.'

6. 'And what about the handle?'

'I don't know. It is yellow, and smooth, and hard.'

'It is bone,' said his uncle, 'part of an ox-bone. But some handles are made of wood.'

7. 'May I look at that knife near you, auntie? I mean the clean one. Thank you!'

8. Then Dora wanted one to look at too; and they felt the edges softly and found them very sharp. They looked at the blunt backs of the blades, and then tried to read the maker's name.

9. 'There is no room to put the maker's name on a needle,' said Harry. 'But how do they get it on here?'

'It is stamped on when the blade is red-hot and rather soft.'

10. They could not make out how the handle was put on, so their aunt went to the knife-box and got out an old knife that had lost its handle. They saw that the blade had a long thin piece of iron at the end of it.

11. 'A long hole is made inside the handle, and this iron thing is put into it, and made fast.'

So their uncle said, and then looked at the clock and saw that it was time for him to go.

Setting out for the Farm.

THE HEN.

bas′-ket	**watch**	**ban′-tams**	**greed′-y**
fetch	**thought**	**know**	**gray**
friends	**charge**	**proud**	**swal′-lowed**
fowls	**pair**	**peck′-ing**	**laughed**

1. The day after Dora and Harry came home, their mother gave them a basket and sent them up to the farm to fetch eggs.

2. Rover went with them, and all three were glad to go, for they had many friends at the farm.

3. There was the great dog, Watch, and there were the cart-horses and the pony, the ducks and the fowls. And there were five girls and boys—Mary, Tom, Johnny, Annie, and Kate.

4. When these five, and Watch, saw Harry, Dora, and Rover coming, they ran down the lane to meet them. They were soon all in the farm-yard, talking as fast as they could talk.

5. Two had to tell about their visit to Needle-town, and five about the doings at the farm, so it was some time before the eggs were thought of.

6. Mary had charge of the eggs, and went every morning to look for new ones.

'Since you went away,' she said, 'I have had a pair of bantams given me, for my very own. Here they are!'

'What little things! and how very pretty!' cried Dora. 'Do they know you, Mary?'

7. 'Yes; I feed them every day. Here comes the big black hen. She has been laying an egg. See how proud she is! She calls out in that way to let the rest know what she has done.'

8. 'Now she is pecking about for food,' said Harry.

Tom said that fowls were always eating.

'They are greedy things,' said Kate.

9. 'Oh, look at this gray hen!' said Harry, 'she picked up a bit of stone just now and ate it! Does she know no better?'

10. 'It is not for food,' Mary told him; 'she takes it to grind up the hard seeds she has swallowed. They all go into a strong little bag, and the stones rub and press on the seeds.'

11. 'I never heard of such a thing! She keeps a mill inside to grind her food!'

12. The others laughed, and then Mary went in to get some eggs. After the basket was filled, the two children said good-bye to their friends, and went home.

THE SPARROW.

shoots	**thou´-sand**	**beaks**	**clean**
spar´-rows	**ba´-bies**	**ap´-ple**	**thirst´-y**
steal	**build**	**blos´-som**	**wheat**
fruit	**spoil**	**fruit**	**throw**

1. 'Mother,' cried Harry, running in one day, 'Jack Denny says he shoots sparrows!'

'I am very sorry to hear it. Why does he shoot them?'

'"They steal fruit and corn," he says. He wanted me to throw stones at them!'

2. 'Well, you can tell him about some silly men who killed the sparrows and other birds, and the next year their fruit and corn were eaten up by grubs. Even the leaves on the trees were eaten.'

3. 'Is this true?'

'Quite true. They had to send for little birds from other places to live in their fields and gardens. Do you know that a sparrow kills four thousand grubs in one day when her babies are in the nest?

4. 'One wise man who grows fruit says that his best friends are the sparrows, and he makes holes in the garden-walls for them to build in. Their sharp eyes see the tiny things that would spoil the fruit, and their sharp beaks nip them up at once.

5. 'He loves to see sparrows in an apple-tree in blossom-time; he knows they are saving the apples for him.'

'But Jack says he has seen them pecking at fruit.'

6. 'Yes, they like fruit, just as you and I do. But there would be no fruit at all, if the birds did not eat the grubs.

7. 'The man I was telling you about puts nets over his trees when the fruit begins to ripen. And I heard only the other day that it is a good plan to put pans of clean fresh water close to the trees and bushes. Then the birds will not go so often to the fruit. They are thirsty and hot, poor things!

8. 'And there would be no corn, if the birds did not kill the wheat-fly's grubs.'

9. When Harry heard all this, he made up his mind not to throw stones at the sparrows, as Jack wanted him to do.

A DAY IN THE COUNTRY.

but′-ter-flies	**flow′-ers**	**pleas′-ant**	**brook′-let**
mer′-ry	**o-bliged′**	**cheese**	**crys′-tal**
gath′-ered	**roamed**	**hedge**	**thrush**
broth′-er	**scoured**	**ease**	**mus′-ic**

1. Where the bees and butterflies
Skim the grassy down,
Four merry little children
Gathered from the town;

2. Ragged little Johnnie,
And his brother Ben,
With wild-flowers are laden,
These merry little men.
Kate and Mat have posies
Of colours bright and gay,
For Tim, their tiny brother,
At home obliged to stay.

3. They have roamed the meadow,
They have scoured the wood,
Seeking nuts and blackberries,
For their pleasant food.
With their nuts and blackberries
And bits of bread and cheese,
On a mossy hedge-bank,
Now they take their ease.

4. Drinking from the brooklet
'Neath the hawthorn tree,
Clear it runs as crystal,
Fresh and bright and free.
And the thrush sings loudly
On the hawthorn spray,
And the brooklet ever
Makes music on its way.

SOME HERBS.

stream	**tea**	**pow´-der**	**pars´-ley**
through	**lett´-uce**	**sprin´-kled**	**thyme**
grav´-el	**tongue**	**flan´-nel**	**herbs**
mar´-ket	**mus´-tard**	**car´-ried**	**sage**

1. A little stream ran through one of the farmer's fields. The water was so clear that you could see the sand and gravel at the bottom, and in it there grew plenty of water-cress.

Water-cress.

2. Harry went one afternoon to help Johnny and Tom to pick it for market, and brought a big bunch home for tea.

3. His mother had picked a lettuce from the garden, and some mustard and

cress, and they were all put on one plate.

'They bite my tongue,' said Dora, 'all but the lettuce. I like it best.'

4. 'And I like the biting,' said Harry. 'Why is this called mustard, mother?'

'Because the yellow mustard comes from it. The seeds are ground to powder.'

'And we eat the leaves. It is a useful plant.'

Lettuce.

5. After tea, mother took some cress-seed and mustard-seed out of two little packets. Then she cut up one or two corks, put them into a deep plate, filled it with water, and sprinkled seed on the cork.

6. 'This is for you, Harry,' she said. 'You will soon have a little crop of mustard and cress. And here is one for Dora!'

In Dora's plate she laid a bit of flannel, poured water on it, and sowed seed. The children carried off their plates to a safe place, and thought it would be fine fun to see roots and leaves come out of the tiny seeds.

7. Then mother called them into the garden to see her parsley. She told them that hares and rabbits would come a long way to feed on a parsley-bed if they could get at it.

8. Close by grew mint, sage, and thyme. 'All these are herbs,' she said. 'They are not like trees, are they?'

'No; they have no bark, no hard wood, and they are so small.'

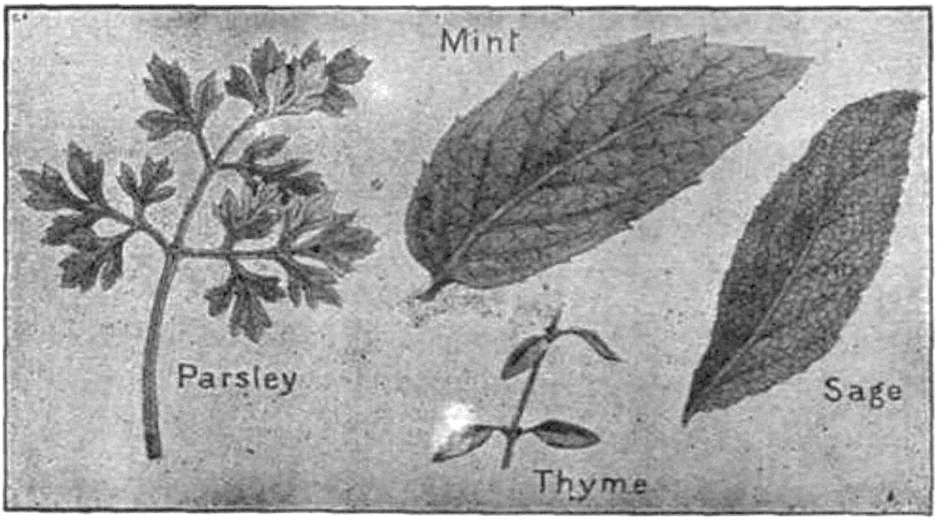

Leaves of Mint, Parsley, Thyme, and Sage.

9. Dora picked a mint-leaf, a parsley-leaf, a thyme-leaf, and a sage-leaf, and laid them side by side. She wanted to see if they were like each other. But when she looked at them she found that they were not alike.

COFFEE.

cof′-fee	**win′-dow**	**rat′-tled**	**blos′-som**
beans	**bus′-y**	**coun′-try**	**cov′-ered**
kneel′-ing	**stock′-ings**	**cher′-ry**	**cloths**
chair	**ket′-tle**	**to-geth′-er**	**ber′-ries**

1. 'What is coffee, mother dear? Does it grow?'

2. It was Dora who asked this. She and Harry were putting away some things that had come from the shop, and she was now filling a tin with coffee-beans.

Coffee branch with Berries.

3. She was kneeling on a chair by the table in the window. Her mother was busy mending stockings, and the cat and the dog were both asleep. The kettle was singing, and all was cosy.

4. The coffee-beans rattled into the tin, and Dora picked one out and looked at it.

When Harry heard Dora asking about it, he also put his hand in and took a coffee-bean. It smelt very nice, he thought. So did Dora.

5. They found that it had a flat side and a round side.

'It humps up,' said Dora.

'See, I can put the flat side of mine against the flat side of yours,' said Harry.

'They grew like that,' said mother.

'Oh, then, they did grow? They were alive once?'

6. 'Yes; they were seeds of a plant that grows in a warm country, far away from here. They once lived inside a berry.

'The berry was red like a cherry, and the seeds inside were held together in a little bag.'

7. 'There must have been a flower before the berry came,' said Harry, thinking of the pea-flower and its pod.

Coffee-flower.

Berry.

Seeds in Berry.

'A very pretty white flower,' said his mother. 'They say that a coffee-garden looks lovely in blossom-time, just as if it were all covered with snow.

8. 'In two or three days the snow-like blossoms are gone, and the fruit is left.

When it is ripe, men put cloths under the trees, and shake it down.'

9. 'I wish I could go and help!' said Harry. 'What comes next?'

'They pick up the berries, dry them in the sun, and get the beans out. Then they send the beans over the sea in a ship. And here they are!'

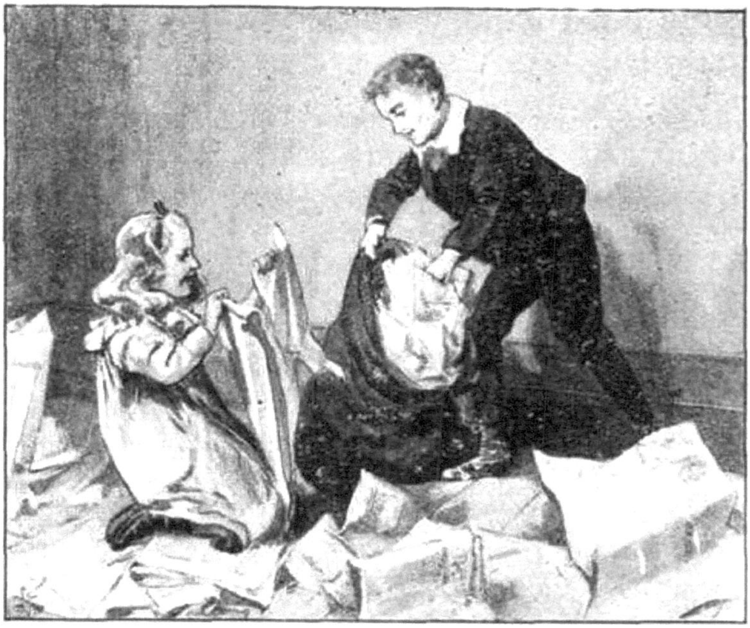

Dora and Harry tearing up the old papers.

PAPER.

un-hap′-py	**per-haps′**	**hearth**	**tear**
should	**clean**	**laugh**	**boil**
tea	**school**	**jok′-ing**	**through**
heels	**clean′-ing**	**in-deed′**	**clev′-er**

1. 'It is such a wet day, I don't know what to do!' said Harry, looking very unhappy.

2. 'Are you tired of your drawing and painting?' asked his mother.

'Oh yes! And we have played at houses, and had the bricks out on the floor, and now there is nothing to do, and it is not nearly tea-time yet. Will you read to us, mother?'

3. 'Not just now. But if you would help me a little I should get on faster, and then we might have a nice time before tea.'

'Jolly!' cried Harry; and he ran to the foot of the stairs and called Dora.

4. Down came Dora very fast, with her doll in her arms, and the dog at her heels.

5. 'What I want you to do,' said mother, 'is to tear up these old papers and put them into this sack. The man is coming soon to take it to the paper-mill.'

6. 'Why is it taken to the paper-mill?' asked Harry.

'To be made over again into paper. Perhaps it will come back to us some day, all clean.

7. 'Or it may be made into a newspaper, and father may bring it home in his pocket.'

'Or we may get it in copy-books at school.'

'Yes; or it may come from the shop with rice in it.'

8. 'It may never come at all,' said Dora. 'Perhaps it will go to some other house.'

'That is quite likely,' said mother, who was now cleaning the hearth.

9. They went on putting the paper into the sack for a long time, and then Harry asked:

'How was paper made before there was old paper to make it of?'

10. 'Oh, it is not made of paper only. It is made of old rags, old ropes'— —

Harry and Dora began to laugh.

'And straw, and wood, and a kind of grass'— —

'Now, are you joking, mother?'

11. 'No, indeed! They cut the wood and straw into tiny bits, and they cut and tear the rags and boil them.'

'And what do they do with the grass?'

'They cut it up, boil it, and mix clay with it. Then it is put through a very clever machine, which makes it into paper.'

A FLY.

spilt	**thirst´-y**	**ceil´-ing**	**won´-der-ful**
won´-der	**mouth**	**ei´-ther**	**straight**
e-nough´	**su´-gar**	**win´-dow**	**count´-ed**
fel´-low	**teeth**	**pane**	**friend**

1. 'Just look here, Harry!' Dora called out.

A little milk had been spilt on the table, and two flies had found it out.

'We won't wipe it up! Let us wait and see if they can take it all. See, it is getting less! I wonder how they do it.'

2. 'There! one fly has gone. He has had enough. But this old fellow is very thirsty. He does not look as if he were drinking, and yet the milk goes. That long thing must be his mouth. Is it, mother?'

3. 'It is called his trunk. The mouth is at the end of it. He is very clever with it. Do you know that he never eats? He only drinks.'

4. 'But I have seen him eating sugar.'

'No; I don't think you have. He has no teeth and no jaws. He can't bite anything. What he does is to wet the sugar with his mouth and melt it, and then suck it up.'

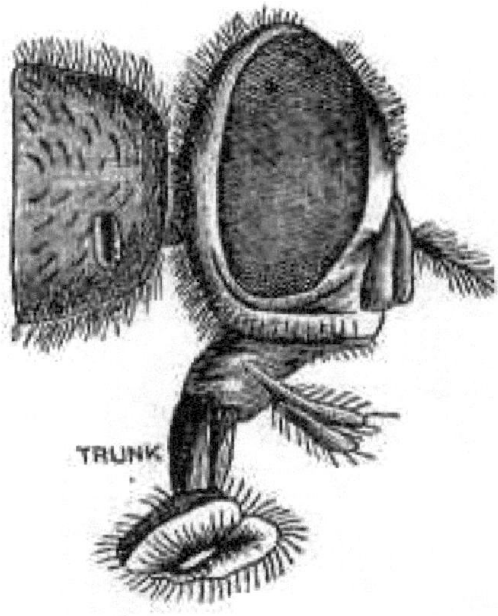

Enlarged view of Head of Fly showing Trunk.

5. 'Well, that is clever! I wonder how he found out how to do it. And I know something else that he is clever at.'

6. 'What is it, Harry?' asked Dora.

'Something you can't do! He can walk on the ceiling.'

'You can't do it either,' said Dora.

'How does he hold on, mother? We can see one up there now! He walks about as if he were on the table.'

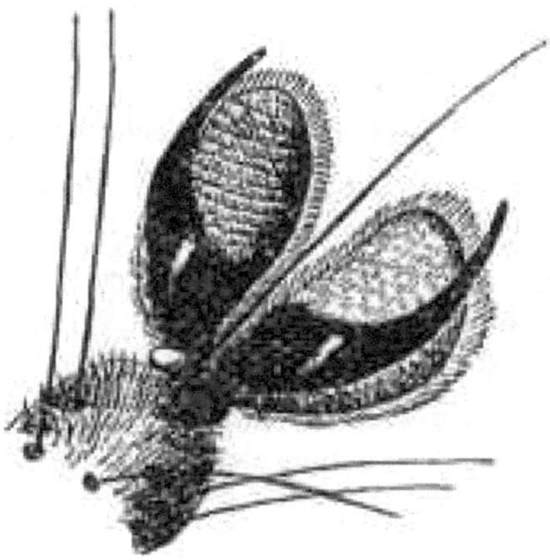

Enlarged view of Fly's Foot.

7. 'He has something like gum inside his feet, and, when he wants to stand or walk upside down, he presses this out, and it helps him to stick on. Here is another fly walking up the window-pane.'

'I have often seen flies on the window-pane.'

8. 'How wonderful it is! The glass, you see, is smooth and hard, and it stands straight up. We could not go up a hill like that, could we?'

9. They watched him go up and down, counted his six legs, and saw that his wings were very pretty. Their mother told them a very strange thing, that his eyes could see all ways at once!

10. Then they had to say good-bye to him, for out he went into the garden. When they turned to the table, they found that their other friend had gone too—and so had the milk.

THE WASP.

wasp	**pass´-age**	**pow´-der**	**pil´-lars**
bus´-y	**loose**	**spread**	**cell**
win´-ter	**per-haps´**	**brown**	**hatched**
ground	**fence**	**comb**	**crawl´-ing**

1. There was a great stir at dinner one day. A wasp came in, begging for sugar and plum-tart. Harry and Dora ran this way and that.

2. At last their father got the wasp out into the garden, and, when all was quiet again, he asked if they would like to hear its story.

'Oh yes, father!' said Dora.

3. Harry was busy with his plums, but he nodded, as much as to say, 'I shall be glad to hear it too!'

4. So the father began:

'All last winter the wasp was asleep, but when spring came she waked up and set out to look for a home. I am not quite sure where she found it, but it was in the ground, I think.

5. 'She began to dig in the soft earth, and she dug on till she had made a long passage. She had to carry out all the loose earth herself. Then she made a little room at the end of the passage.

6. 'Next she looked about for some old wood, and found it in a tree, perhaps, or post, or bit of fence. She rubbed away at it with her jaws till she got some of it off in powder.

7. 'She made this powder into a paste with a sort of gum which came out of her mouth, and off she went with it to her room.'

8. 'What did she do with it?'

'She spread it out in sheets of thin brown paper, and with these she made a comb like a bee's.'

'She made paper of it.'

'Only a bee's is made of wax. I know that!' said Harry.

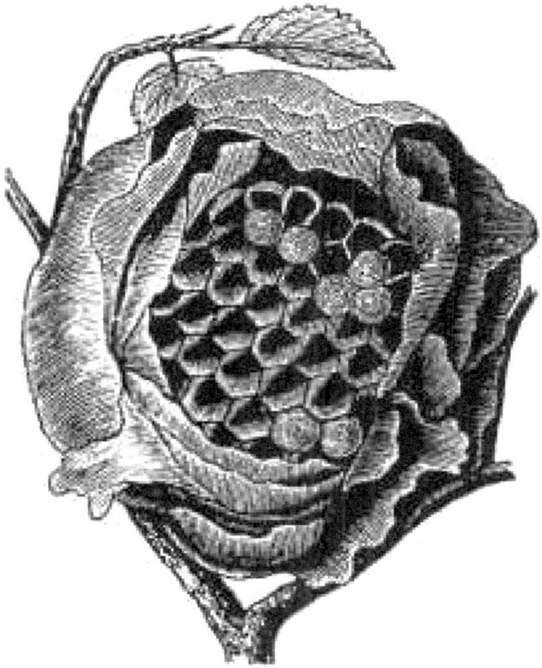

Wasp's Nest.

9. 'She put many layers of paper on the top to keep the rain out, and pillars under it to hold it up. Then she laid an egg in each cell. When the eggs were hatched'——

'Little wasps came flying out,' said Dora.

'No; little grubs came crawling out!

10. 'The wasp was now more busy than ever. She fed each baby in turn, and as they all grew bigger she had to get more and more food for them.'

THE SUNFLOWER.

blue	**sun´-flow-er**	**star´-ing**	**cush´-ion**
buzz´-ing	**course**	**spar-row**	**mid´-dle**
set´-tled	**warmth**	**stopped**	**gar´-den**
watched	**in-stead´**	**crowd**	**know**

1. It was very hot, the sky was blue, and the air was full of the humming and buzzing of bees and flies. A white butterfly flitted by, but soon went away over the garden-wall.

2. Bee after bee, and fly after fly, settled on the sunflowers and hunted for honey. Dora and Harry watched for a long time.

3. 'The sunflower is like a little sun,' said Dora.

'And it loves the sun,' said her mother, who was snipping off dead roses close by; 'it always turns to look at it. See, its face is towards the sun now. And if you look again before sunset you will find the flower turned to it still.'

4. 'How strange!' said Dora.

'And it has such a strong stalk,' said Harry. 'You would not think that it could turn round. It must be alive!'

'Of course it is alive!'

'But, I mean, it must feel, or why should it turn and turn to get the light and warmth?'

5. 'How ragged all the stalks and leaves are!' said Dora. 'I wish they would make themselves tidy instead of always staring at the sun. Why are there so many holes in the leaves?'

6. 'Grubs have been eating them. Our friend Mr Sparrow must have been away lately!'

7. Here mother stopped snipping at her rose-trees, and came up to one of the sunflowers.

8. 'There is something I want you to see,' she said. 'You think this is one big flower, but it is really a crowd of little flowers. Look! Can you think of another flower that is something like it?'

Sunflower.

9. Harry and Dora shook their heads.

'It is very small,' mother went on, 'with a cushion in the middle like this, and rays standing out all round like these.'

10. 'Does it grow on a tree?'

'No.'

'In this garden?'

'No.'

'In the fields?'

'Yes.'

'Oh, I know!' cried Harry. 'It is the daisy.'

MERRY WORKERS.

wheels	**brook′-lets**	**lis′-ten**	**hum′-ming**
bus′-y	**ripp′-ling**	**hon′-ey**	**e-nough′**
i′-dle	**sky′-lark**	**mer′-ri-ly**	**wea′-ry**

1. Tell me what the mill-wheels say,
Always turning night and day;
When we sleep and when we wake,
What a busy sound they make!
Never idle, never still,
What a worker is the mill!

2. What is it that the brooklets say,
Rippling onward day by day?
Sweet as skylark on the wing,
Ripple, ripple—thus they sing.
Never idle, never still,
Always working with a will!

3. Listen to the honey-bee,
Flying now so merrily
Here and there with busy hum—
Humming, drumming, drumming, drum.
Never idle, never still,
Humming, drumming—hum it will!

4. Like the mill, the brook, the bee,
May it now be said of me
That I'm always busy too,
For there's work enough to do.
If I work, then, with a will,
It will be but playing still;
Ever merry, never weary,
It will be but playing still.

THE ROSE.

bas´-ket	**sweet´-ly**	**stooped**	**yel´-low**
wo´-man	**cab´-bage**	**smile**	**a-greed´**
vil´-lage	**be-cause´**	**thorns**	**win´-ter**

1. Mother went back to her roses, and soon called for a little basket, saying that Dora and Harry should take a few to an old woman who lived in the village.

2. 'Poor granny,' she said, 'is so fond of roses, and she can never get out now to see them. Which shall we pick for her?'

3. 'Some of these white ones,' said Dora.

'I think she would like these red ones,' said Harry, 'they smell so sweetly.'

4. Mother cut one or two of each, and then a moss-rose, which looked as if it had moss growing round it, and then a pink cabbage-rose.

Wild Rose.

Garden Rose.

5. 'What has it to do with cabbage?' asked Harry.

'It is only called cabbage because it is so big and round.'

6. 'I like it the best of all,' said Dora, and stooped to smell it, putting her nose far down into the sweet, deep cup: 'it is such a nice rose!'

7. 'Yes, I am very fond of it, and of all roses,' said mother, looking at her bushes with a smile, 'but I almost think I like the wild ones best. Do you know that the wild rose is the mother of all these? Once upon a time all roses were wild.'

8. Harry and Dora did not think that wild roses were very like garden roses. 'But they both have thorns,' they said.

9. 'Look at them as you go along. There are some bushes not far from the bottom of the lane, after you turn round to go to the village. I don't think you will find many roses left, but you will see their fruit. They are the birds' fruit-trees.'

10. 'What can mother mean?' they asked as they went along.

But they soon found out. The bushes were covered with hips; some green, others yellow, one or two quite red.

11. They agreed to leave them for the birds. Dora said 'They would be sure to want them in the winter.'

Making the Doll's House.

WOOD.

min´-er-al	**gummed**	**tools**	**beech**
cop´-per	**climbed**	**dead**	**birch**
zinc	**knees**	**thought**	**wil´-low**
chalk	**eve´-nings**	**oak**	**build´-ing**

1. The little mineral box was made, and Harry and Dora put in the lumps of lead, iron, copper, tin, zinc, chalk, and slate. Father wrote the names on tiny slips of paper and gummed them on.

2. Then he said that he was going to make Dora a doll's house. On hearing this, Dora first jumped about for joy, and then climbed up on her father's knees to kiss and hug him.

3. The doll's house was not made all at once. It had to be done bit by bit in the evenings after father had come home from work and had his tea.

4. Dora and Harry always helped him, or stood by and talked, played with bits of wood, and turned over the tools in the box.

5. They said that saw-dust should be called wood-dust; and they found out that wood was called tree when it was alive, and tree was called wood when it was

dead. They thought this very funny.

6. They also learned that there were as many kinds of wood as there were trees.

'Some wood is hard,' said their father, 'some is half-hard, and some is soft.'

'Soft wood!' cried Dora.

7. 'Well, not soft like butter! But softer than oak, beech, birch, and elm'——

'The trunk of an oak-tree is lying where the rabbits live,' said Harry, in a great hurry. 'We often play on it. I know that it is hard. What sort of wood are you making the doll's house of?'

8. 'Soft wood. It is a bit of pine. So is the box that holds the minerals. I should find it hard work to cut oak.

'Now, there is one kind of wood so soft that you can bend it. It is called willow, and baskets are made of it.

'But oak was once used in building the great strong ships.'

COAL.—PART 1.

win´-dow	**coal**	**won´-der-ing**	**stretch´-ing**
shov´-el	**tum´-bled**	**earth**	**en´-gine**
spade	**con-tent´**	**cage**	**doz´-en**

1. 'Here comes the coal,' said Harry, looking out of the window. 'Mother, may we help Jim to get it in? I can have the big shovel, and Dora the little one. I should like to see the cart upset! What fun it will be!'

2. Crash came the coal on the ground. Then the coal-man drew his horse and cart away, and set to work with a spade to fill the little coal-place.

3. The dog jumped, and got in every one's way. He wanted to help, too, but did not know how. Dora tumbled over the heap and bumped her head, so she thought she would be content with watching Jim and Harry. But Harry was soon tired, and Jim was left to go on alone.

4. 'Where does coal come from, Jim?' he asked.

'Out of the ground, my lad.'

'Does it? Do you dig for it?'

'I don't. But I know somebody who does.'

5. 'If I were to dig for it, should I find any, Jim?'

'Not you! Why, you have to go down ever such a long way before you can even begin to dig.'

6. 'How do you get down?'

'You go down in a thing they call a cage. You can't walk down, you know. It is like going down a deep pit. They call it a mine.'

7. 'Oh, I have heard of coal-mines!'

Dora was taking up one little lump of coal after another, and wondering why it was so shiny if it had really come out of the earth.

8. Harry went on. 'How do they let the cage down? Have you ever been down?'

'I have been down once,' said Jim, stopping in his work and stretching himself. 'This is the way. There is an engine at the top of the shaft'— —

'What is the shaft?'

Coal-miners going down to work.

9. 'The pit I told you about. The engine is fixed there and it lets down the cage and pulls it up again. Half-a-dozen men or so can go in it at a time.'

'It must be very strong.'

10. 'Yes, it is, and it has strong chains to hold it. It goes up and down all day long, bringing up the coal.'

COAL.—PART 2.

re´-al-ly	**knife**	**pic´-tures**	**thou´-sands**
eas´-i-ly	**be-tween´**	**an´-i-mal**	**piec´-es**
slic´-es	**met´-al**	**whole**	**to-geth´-er**
straight	**fetched**	**for´-ests**	**puz´-zles**

1. Next day the children asked their mother to tell them what coal really was. Harry did not think it was a stone, because he had broken two or three lumps with a hammer. He found that it broke much more easily than stone.

2. Besides, it did not fly all into sharp bits, but came off in slices; and he saw that it had straight lines along it. When he poked his knife in between these lines, he could take off a slice of coal at once!

3. Dora did not think it was a metal, because she had learnt that iron would melt in a fire and flow like water. 'Coal does not melt,' she said, 'every one knows that!'

4. She took a small lump out of the coal-box, and Harry did the same. Mother then fetched some pictures, and one or two other things, and the talk began.

5. 'It is no wonder that you can't guess what coal is! It does not look at all like what it was at first. It was not always in the ground; it used to live on the top and get the air and sunshine.'

6. 'It must have been alive,' said Harry. 'Was it an animal?'

'No.'

'Then it was a plant!' cried Dora.

7. 'Well, it is all that is left of many plants and trees, whole forests of plants and trees, that grew long, long ago.'

'Before you were born, mother?'

8. 'Yes, long before that! It was hundreds and thousands of years ago. It was so far back that the trees were not like the trees we have now. Many of them were big ferns. Think of a fern grown up to be a tree! And many were great horse-tails. You know what a horse-tail is?'

9. 'Oh yes,' said Dora, 'we find them in the ditch down the lane. It is such fun pulling them to pieces and putting them together again—like puzzles!'

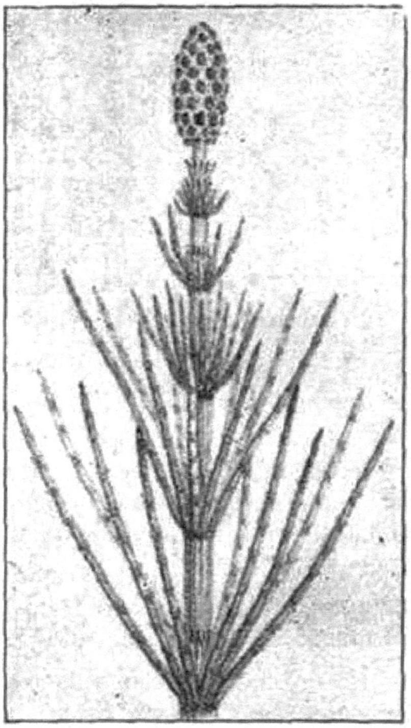

Horse-tail.

10. 'Those trees must have been very strange,' said Harry. 'They would not be nice to climb. But there were no boys in those days, so it did not matter.'

FIRE.

min′-er-al	**walk′-ing**	**Lon′-don**	**blaze**
coal	**laugh′-ing**	**smoke**	**beast**
fen′-der	**grate**	**al-read′-y**	**cage**
prop′-er	**cru′-el**	**flame**	**pic′-tures**

1. 'Don't you think,' said Harry, 'that a bit of coal would be a good thing for our mineral box?'

2. 'I do,' said his father. 'Get a little lump, and put it in. And, by the way, we want more coal on the fire. I must get some.'

3. 'How nice a fire is on a cold day!' said Dora, sitting down on the fender, to be as near to it as she could.

'Very nice,' said her mother, 'in its proper place—in the grate.'

4. 'Ah, we should not like it to come walking about the room!' said Harry, laughing. 'There would soon be no room'——

'And no house!' said Dora, shaking her head. 'And then what should we do?'

5. Father came back with the coal, and put some into the grate, saying:

'Fire is a good servant but a bad master. If it gets its own way it is a cruel thing. It would burn a town down. It once burned big London.'

6. Harry was looking at one of the lumps that had been put on the fire. Smoke was coming out of it already. A flame burst out in front, and soon the whole lump was in a blaze.

7. 'It seems such a pity that it should all be burned up,' said Harry, 'when it took so long to make.'

'That is the way of fire,' said father, 'it eats up everything, and when it has nothing more to feed on it comes to an end—it goes out, we say.'

8. 'We don't want it to go out, and so we keep on feeding it,' said mother. 'It is like a wild beast in a cage.'

'Now look at the coal!' said father.

9. By this time the lumps were red and very hot. The children went down on their knees to look for pictures in the fire. They soon saw what looked like men and dogs, rocks, hills, and trees, and at last a great cat with red-hot eyes and a very curly tail.

OBJECT LESSONS.

THE CAT.

[*Page 1.*

1. The cat lives in and about our homes; so we call it a domestic animal.

2. It belongs to the same tribe of animals as the lion and tiger. They are savage—puss is tame. Like them, it is a beast of prey—that is, it catches and eats other animals. They cannot hear it coming with its soft, padded feet.

3. The cat leaps upon its prey. It sticks its strong, sharp claws into a mouse, and soon kills it with its sharp teeth.

4. Puss is covered with fur; she has five claws on each fore-paw, and four on each hind one. She draws them into little sheaths when not angry.

5. With its rough tongue the cat can lap up milk, and also clean its fur. It likes to be clean. It opens its eyes wider in the dark, and can see to run about at night. On each side of its head are long whiskers, with which it feels its way.

Write and learn:

Cats have—	Cats like—	Cats are—
Padded feet.	Milk.	Domestic.
Sharp claws and teeth.	Meat.	Tame.
Rough tongues.	Mice and rats.	Useful.
Good sight at night.	Birds and fish.	Cleanly.

THE DOG.

[*Page* 5.

1. The dog is larger and more active than the cat. It is also of more use to man, for it guards the house, minds the sheep, and will not allow any one to harm its master.

2. There are many kinds of dogs. All are of some use—from the large Newfoundland dog to the little fox-terrier.

3. Dogs are like cats in some things. They have padded feet and strong claws. But their claws are blunt. They cannot draw them into sheaths as puss does; so they make more noise in walking.

4. The dog is also a beast of prey. But it is not so fierce as the wolf or the fox, which belong to the same tribe of animals. It likes meat and bones, but will also eat bread and vegetables. Its teeth are very strong and sharp.

5. Most dogs have keen scent, pointed noses, and quick sight.

Write and learn:

Dogs have—	Dogs—	Dogs are—
Blunt claws.	Bark.	Useful.
Sharp, strong teeth.	Watch.	Faithful.
Keen scent.	Jump.	Friendly.
Quick sight.	Hunt.	Wise.

BUTTERCUPS.

[*Page 8.*

1. Buttercups grow wild. They are of a golden yellow colour. Each flower has five yellow leaves growing out from the middle of five smaller green ones.

2. The flowers are something like a cup in shape, with a little tuft of grass-like threads standing in each one. In the green ball in the middle there are tiny seeds from which other buttercups will grow if they fall into the ground.

3. Buttercups come in spring. They grow on taller stems than daisies. They have no nice scent such as violets or roses have.

Write and learn·

Buttercups—	Buttercups have—	Buttercups are—
Grow wild.	Five yellow leaves.	Pretty and shiny.
Come in spring.	Five green ones.	Eaten by cattle.

WHEAT.

[*Page 13.*

1. Wheat is a plant of the *grass* kind, but grows higher than common grass. It is grown from seed, which is grains of wheat kept until hard and dry.

2. Ruts are made in the soil by a plough, and into these the seed is cast. Then the soil is covered over them by a harrow, drawn by a horse.

3. Rain and warm sunshine help the grains to grow. They grow into tall, jointed stems, and soon the ears of wheat appear. They are green at first, but the sun ripens them and turns them yellow.

4. Then the wheat is cut, and the new grains are threshed out from the husks which are called chaff. The tall stems make straw. The grains are ground into flour by the miller. We use flour for making bread, cakes, and puddings.

Write and learn:

Wheat is—	Wheat has—	Wheat makes—
A grass plant.	A tall stem.	Flour.
Grown from seed.	Graceful leaves.	Foods.
Green at first.	An ear.	Chaff.
Yellow when ripe.	Grains.	Straw.

SLATE.

[*Page 17.*

1. Slate is a kind of stone. Rocks, and even mountains, are sometimes made of slate. The great hole made in the rocks by getting it out, is called a quarry. It is got out in very large blocks. Sometimes gunpowder is used to crack the rocks before the blocks can be got out.

2. Slate is very hard and brittle. It is used for many purposes. Houses are roofed with slates. Sometimes it is used for pavements. It can be made so smooth that we use it for writing upon. Slate-pencil is made from soft slate-stone.

Write and learn:

Slate is—	Slate is found in—	Slate is useful for—
A kind of stone.	Cumberland.	Roofing houses.
Very hard.	Wales.	Making pavements.
Brittle.	Cornwall and Devon.	Writing upon.

CHALK.

[*Page* 22.

1. Like slate, chalk comes out of the hills. It is white and soft. It is used for many purposes. The farmer puts it on the fields sometimes, to make the soil better. It holds water and keeps the soil moist.

2. We get lime and whiting from chalk. We use it in these forms for making our ceilings and walls clean. It is used, too, for writing on the blackboard. Chalk is found in many parts of England. Kent and Hampshire have most. Chalk-pits are often seen in the hills.

3. Chalk is formed of thousands of tiny shells.

Write and learn:

Chalk is—	Chalk is found in—	Chalk makes—
White.	Hampshire.	Lime.
Soft.	Kent.	Whiting.
Crumbly.	Isle of Wight.	Chalk-pencils.

THE MOUSE.

[*Page 26.*

1. The mouse is a very small animal, with pointed nose and long tail. It has large bright eyes, large ears, strong sharp teeth, and is very timid.

2. The mouse gnaws through the walls and floors of our houses with its sharp, strong teeth. It makes a little nest in a hole. It comes out when all is quiet to look for crumbs, or anything left about that it can eat. It gets into the pantry sometimes.

3. Some mice live in fields and woods. The tiny harvest-mouse makes its nest on a wheat-stalk. It often does great harm to the wheat.

4. But for puss there would soon be so many mice that we should not know what to do.

Write and learn:

Mice have—	Mice like—	Mice are—
Long tails.	Bread.	Very small.
Sharp teeth.	Meat.	Very timid.
Large ears.	Cheese.	Very quick.
Bright eyes.	Milk.	Very quiet.

THE RABBIT.

[*Page 30.*

1. The rabbit is about the size of the cat, and is covered with short fur. It burrows a hole in the ground and makes a nest there for its young.

2. Rabbits have long ears and large eyes. They can hear a very slight sound, and can see *behind* as well as before them.

3. Their hind-legs are longer than their fore-legs; so they do not run, but leap.

4. Rabbits like to live where there is plenty of furze, which they eat for food. They do much mischief in corn-fields by eating the young corn. They also eat the bark off young trees, and so spoil them.

Write and learn:

Rabbits have—	Rabbits eat—	Rabbits—
Long ears.	Grass.	Burrow.
Large eyes.	Roots.	Make nests for their young.
Long hind-legs.	Leaves.	Leap.
Warm fur.	Bark.	Play.

IVY.

[*Page* 32.

1. Ivy is an evergreen, climbing plant. It grows on old walls, houses, and churches, and sometimes on trees.

2. There are several kinds of ivy. The leaves of each kind are of a different shape. All ivy leaves are very pretty.

3. The leaves have little marks called veins, crossing them in all ways. These veins are full of sap, or moisture, which the roots of the plant suck up from the earth.

4. Some ivy flowers, and bears berries.

Write and learn:

Ivy is—	Ivy has—	Ivy grows—
An evergreen.	Different forms of leaf.	On old buildings.
A climber.	Many veins.	Sometimes round trees.

A TREE.

[*Page 34.*

1. There are many kinds of trees. The oak, elm, and beech are very common.

2. Trees have roots, trunks, branches, leaves, and often flowers and fruit. The brown covering of the trunk is called bark. This keeps the tree warm and dry.

3. Their leaves fall off in autumn, except those of evergreens like the holly and the laurel.

4. Trees are both beautiful and useful. They provide us with timber and firewood, and give shade and shelter to our houses and gardens.

Write and learn:

Trees have—	Trees—	Trees give us—
Roots.	Shed leaves.	Timber.
Branches.	Live long.	Fruits.
Leaves.		Shade and shelter.

BRICKS.

[*Page 36.*

1. Bricks are made of clay. The clay is very damp and heavy when it is dug out of the ground.

2. It is put into moulds to make bricks, and slowly baked in a kiln. Then the bricks are dry and not so heavy as the clay was. They are porous.

3. Most bricks are of oblong shape. This is the shape used for building houses, schools, walls. Sometimes they are made into very pretty shapes, are glazed and used for floors and other things.

Write and learn:

Bricks are—	Bricks are—	Bricks are used—
Made of clay.	Not so heavy as stone.	For building.
Shaped in moulds.	Hard.	For ornament.
Baked in a kiln.	Oblong.	

THE DONKEY.

[*Page 38.*

1. The donkey is a useful animal when well treated. It is cheaper to buy and to keep than a pony.

2. The donkey has hoofs like the horse, and wears shoes. It is very patient and gentle, and can do with coarse food.

3. The donkey's coat is rough, and its mane short. It has a black stripe down its back and across its shoulders. Its head and ears are very long.

4. The donkey can climb high rugged paths better than the horse. It can also carry heavy loads up hill, because it is strong and sure-footed.

Write and learn:

The donkey has—	The donkey is—	The donkey likes—
Hoofed feet.	Strong.	Hay.
Long ears.	Sure-footed.	Grass.
A shaggy coat.	Gentle.	Thistles.
A short mane.	Patient.	Carrots.

SHEEP.

[*Page 40.*

1. Sheep live mostly in the fields. They often climb very high hills. Their feet are not like the donkey's; they are cloven, like the cow's.

2. Their legs are so slender that their bodies seem almost too large for them. The thick wool which grows upon them makes them look large.

3. Sheep eat grass. They tear it off, as the cow does. They cannot bite, since they have no front teeth in the upper jaw.

4. They are very timid, gentle creatures. They do not like to be alone. They live in flocks. They make a great noise when bleating.

5. Sheep are very useful. Their flesh gives us mutton; their wool makes clothing; their skin makes leather.

Write and Learn:

Sheep have—	Sheep are—	Sheep give us—
Cloven hoofs.	Gentle.	Food.
Slender legs.	Timid.	Clothing.
Thick wool.	Climbers.	Leather.

TURNIPS.

[*Page* 43.

1. Turnips are grown both in fields and gardens. The tops are green. The turnip is almost round; but it tapers towards the bottom. Most of the turnip grows under ground; but we can see part of it above ground when nearly ripe.

2. Turnips are good for food. Sheep and cattle are fond of them. Animals eat them raw. We boil them. Raw turnips are not good for us. Pigs will eat the rinds which we peel off.

3. Turnips are white or yellow, sweet, juicy, wholesome.

Write and learn:

Turnips are—	Turnips have—	Turnips are eaten—
White or yellow.	Roots.	By man.
Sweet.	Green tops.	By animals.
Wholesome.	Thick rinds.	Mostly in winter.

GREEN PEAS.

[*Page 45.*

1. The pea is a climbing plant. We put tall sticks in the garden for the peas to climb. They grow from seeds which are dried peas.

2. As they grow, tendrils shoot out and take hold of the sticks. Pretty green leaves grow too. Then come the dainty white flowers.

3. When the flowers wither, they leave little green pods. Inside the pods are little green peas. Peas and pods grow larger each day until ripe.

4. Peas are very good for food. Pigs like the husks.

Write and learn:

Peas have—	Peas—	Peas grow—
Roots.	Climb.	In gardens.
Tendrils.	Grow from seed.	In fields.
Flowers.	Hold by tendrils.	In summer.

IRON AND METAL.

[*Page 49.*

1. Metals are made from ores which are dug out of the earth. These ores are found in many parts of the world. Iron is the most common, as well as the most useful metal.

2. Many things we use are made of it. The *steel* of which our knives, tools, and other things are made, is made from iron. Iron is largely used for making bridges, railings, fire-grates, hammers.

3. Lead, copper, tin, and zinc are metals also. So are silver and gold.

4. Men must dig deep down into the earth to find them. The holes and passages which they make are called mines.

5. All metals are heavy. All will melt in great heat, and all can be hammered out into thin sheets or drawn out into wire.

Write and learn:

Metals are—	Metals can be—	The common metals are—
Heavy.	Melted.	Iron.
Useful.	Hammered out.	Lead.
Plentiful.	Polished.	Tin and copper.

NEEDLES.

[*Page 52.*

1. Needles are made of steel wire. In a needle-factory there are hundreds of coils of wire. Some of the wire is thick enough for darning-needles; some very thin for making sewing-needles.

2. The wire is cut by a machine. The needles are pointed on a grindstone. The eyes are punched by another machine. Then the needles are filed to make them smooth.

3. To make them hard, the needles are made white-hot, and put into cold water until quite cool. They are then cleaned and polished.

4. They must be very dry before put into packets, or they will rust.

5. Many boys and girls, as well as men and women, work in needle-factories.

Write and learn:

Needles are—	Needles have—	Needles are used—
Smooth.	Eyes.	For sewing.
Bright.	Shanks.	For darning.
Pointed.	Points.	For other work.

THE KNIFE.

[*Page* 59.

1. A knife is most useful for cutting. The blade is made of steel; the handle of ivory, bone, or wood.

2. The blade and handle are fastened together by a long, thin piece of iron which goes into the handle. The blades have to be heated as needles are, to make them hard.

3. A knife is blunt on one edge; sharp on the other. The grinder sharpens it on a huge stone which goes round and round. The blades are polished before being put into the handles, as well as after.

4. There are many kinds of knives. Pocket-knives have a spring to make them shut tightly. A table-knife is rounded at the end; the carving-knife has a sharp pointed blade.

Write and learn:

Knives are—	Knives have—	Knives are made—
Sharp.	Blades.	In Sheffield.
Bright.	Handles.	
Useful.	Springs.	

THE HEN.

[*Page 61.*

1. The hen is a domestic bird. Some are white; some black; others many colours. The hen finds much of its own food in the fields. It is fed with barley, bread, potatoes, and other things from the house.

2. The hen has a small head with eyes at the sides. Its bill is strong and sharp.

3. The hen sleeps on a perch on one leg. It never falls off; its foot is made for grasping.

4. Hens are useful for the eggs they give us; and they are also good for food. Their feathers, too, are useful.

Write and learn:

The hen has—	The hen is—	The hen gives us—
A small head.	A domestic bird.	Eggs.
A strong bill.	A percher.	Food.
A grasping foot.	Useful.	Feathers.

THE SPARROW.

[*Page* 63.

1. The sparrow is a small bird with brown and gray feathers. It builds its nest on our houses, and sometimes in the pipes which carry the rain off the roof. A sparrow's nest is seldom found in a tree. It lays five or six eggs which are spotted with brown.

2. Farmers often kill sparrows because they steal the corn and fruit. But they are really good friends to the farmer. They eat the worms and grubs, which would destroy *all* the fruit.

3. The sparrow is a very bold little bird, and is to be found in the streets of the largest towns as well as in the country.

Write and learn:

The sparrow has—	The sparrow is—	The sparrow eats—
Brown and gray feathers.	Small.	Grain.
Sharp claws.	Bold.	Worms.
A long tail.	Useful.	Fruit.

HERBS.

[*Page 67.*

1. Herbs are plants or vegetables with soft stalks or stems. Some grow wild, others we grow in our gardens.

2. We use some for eating, such as mustard and cress. Others, such as parsley, mint, sage, and thyme, we use to flavour our food. Many are used as medicine.

3. Most herbs have a nice scent. They are very plentiful, and very useful.

Write and learn:

Herbs have—	Herbs are—	Herbs are used—
Soft stems.	Plentiful.	For eating.
Nice scent.	Useful.	For flavouring.
Strong flavour.	Grown from seeds.	For medicine.

COFFEE.

[*Page 70.*

1. We get coffee from the coffee-tree. It is an evergreen, something like our bay-tree. It bears a pretty white flower.

2. When the flower falls it leaves a red berry, something like a cherry. The two hard, oval seeds inside it are what we call coffee beans. They are of a pale colour in the berry, but are roasted to make them brown.

3. Coffee is good to drink, but it is not so cheap as tea. It grows in warm countries far away—in Arabia and the West Indies chiefly.

Write and learn:

The Coffee-tree—	Coffee is—	Coffee grows—
Is an evergreen.	Good to drink.	In Arabia.
Has white flowers.	Warming.	In the West Indies.
Has a red berry.	Not so cheap as tea.	In Brazil.

PAPER.

[*Page 73.*

1. Paper is one of the most useful things we have. It is made of old rags which are torn to pieces by a machine. Lime is put in to make them white.

2. The pulp, as it is called, is then formed into sheets and pressed. It is then covered with *size,* and pressed again to make it smooth and glossy.

3. Blotting-paper and other kinds not used for writing upon, are not sized. Brown paper is made of old canvas and sacking.

4. Before paper was made, people used to write upon the inner bark of trees, and the thin skins of animals made sweet and dry, and called parchment.

Write and learn:

Writing-paper is—	Blotting-paper is—	Brown paper is—
Smooth.	Soft.	Coarse.
Glossy.	Unglazed.	Strong.
Fine.	Porous.	Used for parcels.

THE FLY.

[*Page 75.*

1. The fly is a wonderful little insect. It has six legs, with such curious feet that it can walk on the window-panes or the ceiling.

2. It has a funny little round head. Its eyes stand out so that it can see round about it. It cannot move its eyes as we do. Neither can it bite its food—it sucks it.

3. The fly teases us in summer. It gets into our sugar, milk, treacle, and honey. Then it makes marks upon our windows and other things.

4. Its wings are very pretty. When they get wet it cannot fly. The noise flies make is called buzzing.

Write and learn:

Flies have—	Flies—	Flies like—
Six legs.	Buzz.	Sugar.
Curious feet.	Lay tiny eggs.	Honey.
Fixed eyes.	Suck their food.	Milk.

THE WASP.

[*Page 78.*

1. A wasp is a very pretty insect, black and yellow in colour. There are several kinds. Some burrow in the ground and make their nests there. Others build their nests in trees.

2. Wasps live together in large numbers. They are very busy. Some lay eggs; some are masons, and build the nest; others are soldiers, and guard the home; whilst others carry away all the rubbish, and keep everything clean and tidy.

3. The wasp's sting has poison in it. This is why it gives us such pain if we get stung.

4. The wasp is something like the fly in shape, only much larger. It preys upon other insects.

Write and learn:

The Wasp has—	The Wasp—	The Wasp likes—
Six legs.	Makes a nest.	Insects.
Four wings.	Works hard.	Meat.
A sharp sting.	Sleeps all winter.	Sweet things.

THE SUNFLOWER.

[*Page 80.*

1. This flower is called *sun*-flower because it always turns its face to the sun. It turns as the sun goes round.

2. The sunflower grows on a strong, tall stalk. It is something like a daisy in form.

3. The deep-yellow leaves stand out in rays from the dark-coloured middle of the flower, which is called the *disk*. This disk is made of a large number of tiny flowers closely packed together.

4. The seeds of this flower are large and oblong, and contain oil.

5. Bees and flies visit sunflowers, to gather honey.

Write and learn:

The sunflower has—	The sunflower—	The sunflower has—
A strong stalk.	Grows from seed.	Small flowers in its disk.
A large disk.	Contains honey.	Oblong seeds.
Many rays.	Turns to the sun.	Oily seed.

THE ROSE.

[*Page 83.*

1. Roses are of many kinds and many colours. Most of them are sweet-scented. Some rose-bushes do not grow very high. Others grow up as high as our houses.

2. Roses have thorns on their stems. Wild roses have many thorns. Wild roses are small—have only five leaves—but they are very pretty.

3. When they die they leave berries, called hips, which make good food for the birds in winter. There are seeds in them.

Write and learn:

The rose has—	The rose is—	The wild rose—
A sweet scent.	Sometimes white.	Grows in hedges.
Sharp thorns on its stem.	Sometimes yellow.	Has five leaves.
Soft, smooth leaves.	Sometimes red.	Has berries called 'hips.'

WOOD.

[*Page 85.*

1. Wood seems to be almost as useful as iron. Hundreds of years ago, houses were built of wood. All the houses in London were. There is much wood in our houses now.

2. There are many kinds of wood—each comes from a different tree. Oak is a very hard wood. Pine is softer. Willow is very soft; its thin branches will bend easily. It is used for making baskets.

3. When the trunk of a tree is sawn into planks we can see the grain or marks in it. Some are very prettily marked. Oak and walnut are. Wood can be highly polished.

Write and learn:

Wood grows—	Wood is—	Wood is used for—
In most countries.	Very useful.	Building purposes.
In forests.	Mostly hard.	Furniture.
Plentifully.	Grained.	Fires.

COAL.

[*Page 87.*

1. Coal is dug out of the earth. Coal and iron are found together. But coal is not a metal as iron is. It will not melt. We call it a mineral.

2. It is found in many parts of the world. There is a very large quantity in our own country.

3. It is a black, shiny, opaque, and brittle mineral. Men have to go deep down into the earth, into mines, to get it. They are in great danger.

4. Coals were once forests, which sank lower and lower into the earth hundreds and thousands of years ago. They became mixed with other things, and in time were changed to coal. We can see the grain in some of the coal, as we see it in wood.

Write and learn:

Coal is—	Coal is—	Coal is used for—
A Mineral.	Buried forests.	Fuel.
Black.	Got from mines.	Smelting metals.
Opaque.	Heavy.	Making gas.
Brittle.	Grained.	Making tar.

FIRE.

[*Page 91.*

1. Fire is useful but dangerous. A spark from it might set a house on fire. We ought to be very careful about it. Children should never play with fire.

2. It is so useful that we should not be able to have many things we have, if we had no fire.

3. When England was covered with forests, hundreds of years ago, people used to have fires of wood, instead of coal. Wood-fires are not so smoky as those made of coal, but they are not so hot.

Write and learn:

Fire is—	Fire—	Fire—
Useful.	Burns.	Warms our houses.
Dangerous.	Smokes.	Cooks our food.
A good servant.	Makes flame.	Makes water into steam.
A bad master.	Gives heat.	Makes soot.

THE END.

Lector House believes that a society develops through a two-fold approach of continuous learning and adaptation, which is derived from the study of classic literary works spread across the historic timeline of literature records. Therefore, we aim at reviving, repairing and redeveloping all those inaccessible or damaged but historically as well as culturally important literature across subjects so that the future generations may have an opportunity to study and learn from past works to embark upon a journey of creating a better future.

This book is a result of an effort made by Lector House towards making a contribution to the preservation and repair of original ancient works which might hold historical significance to the approach of continuous learning across subjects.

HAPPY READING & LEARNING!

LECTOR HOUSE

LECTOR HOUSE LLP

E-MAIL: info@lectorhouse.com

9 789356 146846

9 789356 146846

Printed by Libri Plureos GmbH in Hamburg,
Germany